I Believe in You

Published by New City Press
202 Comforter Blvd.,
Hyde Park, NY 12538
www.newcitypress.com

Cover design and layout by Miguel Tejerina

I Believe in You
Library of Congress Control Number: 2018960038

ISBN: 978-1-56548-348-4 (paperback)
ISBN: 978-1-56548-361-3 (e-book)

I Believe in You

Wisdom from community with persons with disabilities on believing in ourselves and the other

Luca Badetti

Revised Edition

New City Press
Hyde Park, New York

To the community of loved ones that was there for me in March of 2017 when the unexpected happened.

True ordinariness is tangible holiness. *I Believe in You* by Luca Badetti is an invitation to embrace this beautiful reality by experiencing within ourselves the liberating power of love, simplicity, surrender and trust, inspired by the book's messages and the stories from the community of L'Arche present in its pages. Time spent with this book welcomes us to relax with our authentic selves in an age marked by narcissism and doubt. As you travel with Badetti to uncover life's meaning "in unexpected places" outside of ourselves, each chapter will encourage you to find essential value in yourself in surprising places as well. This gentle, prophetic, heartfelt work is worthy of reflection... and prayer. He has given us a psychological and spiritual gift at a time in society when we most need it.

Robert J. Wicks
Author of *Night Call*

This beautiful book is about becoming who we are, with stories from the amazing community of L'Arche, one of the great Christian ministries of our age.

James Martin, SJ
Author of *Between Heaven and Mirth*

I found this book to be a true eye-opener. Through narratives with a community of persons with and without disabilities, it encourages us to encounter ourselves and others in a way that can deepen our spirituality.

David Richo
Author of *How to be an Adult*

"The stance of tenderness—that loving respect made manifest in gentleness—can free us to be who we are," reads one of the many quotes in Luca Badetti's book, *I Believe in You.*
Living in relationship in community with the so-called intellectually disabled, Luca tenderly unveils his own growth

and evolving inner transformation inspired by stories from those very housemates! Luca, with depth and conviction, further invites you and me to tenderly search the stumbling complexities of our own inner lives, mostly in relationship to ourselves, but also to others, so as to free who we truly are. *I Believe in You* engenders serious introspection but also validates the exquisite gifts of those so often marginalized by those of us who fear the challenges of becoming more truly human.

Sue Mosteller, CSJ
Executrix of Henri Nouwen's literary estate

Luca Badetti's thoughtful book is a gentle and valuable reminder to those of us who struggle with feeling "good enough" to be loved—just as we are with our strengths and weaknesses, abilities and limitations—that each of us is lovable as people uniquely fashioned by divine Love. He shares the "life wisdom" he has gained through living in community with people with disability—valuable lessons of living without pretense, trusting in our innate goodness, and sharing life in interdependent relationships.

Wilkie Au
Author of *God's Unconditional Love*

Are you finally ready to believe in you? Are you ready to claim your own beauty and goodness? In *I Believe in You* Dr. Luca Badetti invites you to discover you are worth being known and celebrated. Written in a warm, calm, personal style, Dr. Badetti shares significant narratives that, stemming from a unique community that has much to teach us about finding and offering ourselves, embody what it means to be(come) fully human, fully alive, and fully being. You must read this book.

David Arute
Professional Counselor, Co-President of The Mansio Center

Badetti has written a wonderful book which explores the question of belief – how we believe in ourselves, in others and in God. The L'Arche community members with whom he lived were his inspiration and teachers, helping him to learn who we all are: God's beloved. This book is a very profound human story of acceptance. Through stories, it shows us how to truly be present, listen and understand ourselves and the other. It challenges our view of those outside of our "comfort zone" and invites us to let down our barriers to celebrate what it is to be truly human.

Ronald Rolheiser, OMI
President, Oblate School of Theology
Author of *The Holy Longing*

A precious and much-needed book. A lot of our personal and social issues stem from not trusting our innate value and, consequently, that of our fellow human beings. The relevant insights and inclusive stories in these pages can help us believe and grow in our humanity, healing our relationship with ourselves and our relationships with others.

Helen Prejean, CSJ
Author of *Dead Man Walking*

In the spirit of the Gospels Luca Badetti's book, *I Believe in You*, takes us on a spiritual journey that opens our hearts to trust in ourselves, which as he says, "is not about achieving something, but about receiving the gift of our being." He has cut through to the heart of the spiritual life. "Receiving the gift of our being" is both the challenge and the gift of spiritual living. And he does this with gentle sincerity by inviting us to encounter, in these pages, members of his L'Arche community and, in our lives, those that are often marginalized. This leaves us with a profound experience of Divine Presence at the heart of our being.

Ken Sedlak, CSsR
Author of *Why God Loves Us...No Matter What*

In this poignant book, Luca Badetti is sharing lessons and insights learned about life from his friends with disabilities in the community of L'Arche. By Luca's willingness to be open to them, they have become true teachers, teaching him not so much about people with disabilities but about the essence of what it means to be human, to accept ourselves, and to be open to the grace and wonder that can come from relationships with others, especially those on the margins. Simply, in understanding them, we understand ourselves. With elegance and simplicity, Luca Badetti invites us into that journey.

Bill Gaventa, MDiv
Founder of the *Summer Institute on Theology and Disability*

People from different walks of life and backgrounds can find, in this book, fresh and novel insights into their individual and social development, as Luca Badetti shares experiences and reflections from living in a diverse community of people with and without intellectual disabilities. Insightful, yet easy to read, informative yet accessible, this is a book for the journey.

Tamar Heller
Distinguished Professor and head of the
Department of Disability and Human Development
(University of Illinois at Chicago)

An inspiring and thought-provoking work that reveals hope in humanity.

Brian Schmisek
Author of *The Apostles' Creed: Articles of Faith for the 21st Century*

Contents

Preface

This book is fundamentally about trust and, as I sit writing, trust is severely tested on a global scale. A pandemic is taking place internationally, with social distancing and caution needed; during a pandemic anyone could be considered a possible threat. Beyond the specifics of this public health emergency, as well as beneath the fears and anxieties associated with it, we may be surprised to find abiding human needs, questions and desires that touch the very core of our humanity: our personhood so deeply linked to our vulnerability, the balance between being alone and being with others, our wanting to trust that ultimately all shall be well even if the circumstances are difficult.

These fundamental human issues have accompanied civilization throughout time, as people consistently tried to make sense of life and grappled with belief. Philosophies have suggested various meanings to life: happiness, pleasure, knowledge, and ethical living. Religions have opened the search to a wide horizon, seeing love of God, communion with people, detachment from materialism, and respect for creation as spiritual components without which the human person suffocates. The sciences have developed sophisticated healing practices, both physical and psychological.

This book seeks to help you believe in yourself and to believe in others. Although belief is often associated with God or a set of concepts, it can be easy to forget how primary and essential belief in ourselves and in each other can be. We can search in high places for big answers, often failing to see what is right next to us and within us, in the little stories and experiences that make up our lives and provide meaning "from the ground up."

To believe means to trust. This is true etymologically, but most essentially it is a reality that can be experienced. What does trust mean and how does it manifest itself? Do we believe, or trust, in ourselves? Who are we in the first place? Do we believe, or trust, in others?

As individuals, we might take for granted that we know who we are until we start questioning our identity. Some people identify with societal statuses, professional roles, geographic location or other markers that give them a sense of who they are, only to feel alienated from that identity once such markers are threatened (the end of a relationship, the loss of a job, a move to another country and so forth). Some have found identity in deeper places, even if to some extent every human being remains a mystery to themselves.

As relational beings, we may have connections with few or many people — deep and rich connections, or superficial and fleeting ones. Our sense of belonging might be centered or stretched in different directions. Our being might hold contrasting histories: experiences of feeling valued and cherished, but also experiences of feeling unwanted and hurt.

Unfortunately, trust is not always respected — in families, in communities, in churches, in schools, in workplaces, and in other places. There are stories of rejection, abuse and neglect in the world. May justice be done and healing happen. In families, communities, churches, schools, workplaces, and other places there are also many stories of trust respected, of trust flourishing, of trust liberating. May love show the way and unity be fostered.

I hope this book will help you grow wherever you are at in your trust path. The reflections presented in the next pages do not come primarily from my readings of heady philosophers, important theologians, or interesting psychologists, but from my journey alongside people with and without intellectual disabilities in community, where transformative wisdom and insight may be found.

Life often presents its meaning in unexpected places, quietly whispered through the "littleness" that people easily forget, overlook, or bypass, busying themselves with loftier thoughts, bigger plans, and quicker answers.

Francis of Assisi found meaning by stripping himself of riches and finding value in the sun, the moon, the rain, and other elements of creation; Mother Teresa found God among lepers and others discarded by society; Gandhi responded to the noisy arrogance of war by proposing the simple humanness of nonviolent encounters; Nelson Mandela lived a fulfilling life while enduring many years confined in a prison cell because of his belief in the diverse unity of the human family.

In L'Arche ("The Ark" in English) communities across the world, people with and without intellectual disabilities, from different religions, cultures, and backgrounds dwell together as housemates or work-mates, and live out a spirituality of community, with the opportunity of finding meaning by accepting their abilities and inabilities, while discovering acceptance and belonging.

The scriptural image of God choosing the "foolish of the world" to confound those deemed "wise" (1 Cor. 1:27, NRSV) and the exhortation to become friends with the poor, the crippled, the lame, and the blind (Lk 14:13) can remind us that, even if today we use different language, those that are often marginalized should be at the center of the social milieu, not at its margins. We might even discover that the descriptors used in Luke's Gospel are not merely categories of people "out there," but states of being we all share.

To some it might seem novel that people with intellectual disabilities can lead us on the path of believing in ourselves and in others. Throughout history, in fact, society has generally not believed in them in the first place: they have often been treated as not fully human, consistently pushed aside, their voices silenced and their wisdom stifled. Their place should not be at the margins of society but at the center, alongside people without intellectual disabilities.

In L'Arche homes, people live inclusively and cook, eat, pray, play, clean, go on outings, rest, watch TV, and live the ordinariness of human life with a quiet love that is ready to celebrate and forgive people through their ups and downs. In L'Arche, people with intellectual disabilities are called "core members" because they are at the heart (the core) of community life. Each community is usually comprised of a few group (or better, community) homes, in which core members live together with people without intellectual disabilities who come to share life with them as live-in assistants or volunteers. The term "sharing life" (or "sharing time") better highlights the relational quality lived by assistants and core members as compared to "working with" or "being on the schedule," even though assistants are asked to fulfill work responsibilities as direct care support workers. Core members are generally invited to make L'Arche their home for life, but assistants tend to transition. Some come to live in L'Arche for a year, some stay longer.

I first joined L'Arche in 2007 as a live-in assistant. Although I had little previous experience with people who have disabilities, I can see how throughout my own personal history I developed a sensitivity and attention towards people that were rejected. I was born in Italy and have beautiful memories of growing up at the Roman seaside with great childhood friends. Even at a young age I exhibited an interest in people considered somewhat "different" and at the margins.

Around my middle school years, I moved to the northern Italian city of Milan and then to the United States; as a friendly and sensitive person, I tasted a bit of what it meant to be different and not in the "mainstream." During middle school I had interests quite different from other people my age and as a high school teenager I used to sit in the cafeteria with other foreigners like me that had come to the United States and were going through the school's English as a Second Language program. Together we communicated through gestures and broken English.

During college, once I had already become more fluent in English, I met new friends with whom I could communicate more easily. I undertook studies in a variety of disciplines as I sought to study and understand the human person in a wholistic way, aware that different fields of study point to various interconnected elements of human reality. Within me, I noticed a growing awareness that being close to the margins of reality, in community with those who are rejected, sheds a light on the meaning of life.

I learned about L'Arche through reading and community visiting. I sensed an interior invitation to join L'Arche as a school of life. Through the years, I have been involved in various L'Arche communities in both the United States and Europe (in this book, however, for ease of reading, they will not be differentiated but will all be grouped and referred to as one community). I have taken on various roles in the community, including being a volunteer, live-in assistant and director of community life. Besides the different responsibilities each role carried, however, one consistent thread remained: I wanted to be in community with people with intellectual disabilities. Even though my academic endeavors led to a doctorate in Disability Studies, what I learned from living in community alongside them goes beyond what one can learn from books. In a society obsessed with reason, control, and independence, they have a prophetic gift that can highlight the primacy of the heart, the courage of trust, and the significance of interdependence, values that are profoundly human and therefore simply divine.

In this book I have tried to strike various balances. Although the book is based on examples and stories from community life, it should have value for a general audience. It is intended for people with little or no exposure to the reality of disability, as well as for those who are close to the experience of disability, whether personally or through their involvement with others. I therefore invite a widely inclusive readership to embark along these pages.

Secondly, this book seeks to draw inspiration from true stories involving core members without stereotyping people with disabilities as inspirational objects. The core members mentioned here are real subjects, adults that—like anyone else—have their ups and downs, joys and struggles, light and shadow sides. Popular representations of disability typically tend to be extreme and inaccurate—on one side the "disability is bad and sad" tear-jerker pietistic approach, on the other the saccharine "people with disabilities are so innocent and always happy" emphasis. Neither of these attitudes considers their unique individuality and human complexity as people. Stories of individuals with disabilities in the media often emphasize how they succeed in living despite the obstacles their impairments present, but this "super-hero" approach tends to equate disability with individual suffering, without showing how disabling and painful external social barriers and prejudices can be.

The stories presented in the next pages are all profoundly relational. I believe people with intellectual disabilities do have a special gift that can help transform society so that it becomes more human. I have found inspiration in this, but I have also found inspiration in the people without intellectual disabilities who live community with them. They, too, are included here. This stance challenges the "us versus them" concerning people with disabilities. It is true that we are healed by the marginalized and rejected, but healing invites us to develop inclusive encounters, and not to unjustly keep whoever is differently grouped on the fringes of society.

These reflections are based on my experiences in community, but I seek to connect them to your own life experience, with the hope that they can speak to you and, as you bring them in dialogue with your life, provide new insights to support your personal and relational growth. Not everyone is called to join L'Arche or other similar communities, yet the "heart" of what is found in this way of life needs to be shared widely, as it can truly speak to all. Ultimately, I would like this book to be of help to you, the reader, in discovering what it means to believe in yourself and in others. I would like to offer these stories and reflections while encouraging to take what speaks to you and to leave what doesn't, possibly after engaging with it.

In presenting these reflections I won't stop at storytelling but will also share insights from psychology, theology and philosophy, which I explored through interdisciplinary studies. Drawing from these different disciplines helps me connect the stories at the basis of this book to various layers of the human experience.

Although L'Arche draws quite a bit from Catholic spirituality, its practice is also ecumenical and inter-faith. As it spread around the world and welcomed people from different spiritual paths and religious traditions (but also those who do not identify with any of them), it has grown and learned through inclusive openness. As a Catholic, I have been honored to live in community alongside Christians of other denominations, Jews, Muslims, Buddhists, agnostics, and atheists. Living a spirituality of togetherness and inclusion can only be done among people who are different. This book seeks to reflect this universality by including, alongside references from the tradition I am familiar with (the Christian one), voices from other paths as well.

I am directing the reflections here to each singular reader, but we are on this journey together. Although we have different histories, experiences, beliefs, and understandings, what is most personal can truly be what is most universal, as Nouwen pointed out.[1] The struggles and joys that we face on the road of trusting in ourselves are profoundly individual, yet at the core they are also intensely human.

In the next pages we will meet Jennifer, Jacob, Leo, Karen, and other L'Arche core members (and assistants). All the stories are true and all the people I write about are real, with some specific information (for example, individuals' names) changed in the narrative. I hope this time together will help us believe in ourselves and in others, finding personal wholeness in our being and unity with those around us, through the wisdom of those that too often have not been believed in.

Introduction

One evening, after a community event attended by almost fifty people, I took a seat next to Jennifer, an outgoing woman of gregarious spirit, genuine affection, and deep spirituality, who has Down syndrome. That evening I was feeling a little low and, as people around us were getting ready to leave the event, I turned to Jennifer to chat for a bit. She is a woman who treasures her faith, and I wanted to talk to her about God and the questions and challenges to belief that I was facing at that moment. I felt the need to share this with her but, considering that we were in a big noisy room surrounded by the distraction of people coming and going, I was not expecting a long conversation. Maybe, however, she would listen and possibly even reply with a word of wisdom, from her own faith experience. I began saying, "You know, I believe in God, but…" Before I finished my sentence, she interrupted me in the low tone of voice she uses when speaking about something serious and replied, "I believe in you…I believe in you," repeating those words twice as she looked at me from behind her glasses. Just after these words something got her attention and she began getting ready to leave. "I believe in you," were the words she left me with.

Jennifer's clear and unexpected affirmation re-directed me to wonder within whether I believed in myself in the first place, or how much I did, even before any inner question about my faith in God. Jennifer turned my question about belief in God into an affirmation of myself. She believed in me. Did I believe in myself?

Jennifer's tone in affirming her belief in me was surely not like one of those cliché motivational slogans that invite people to believe in their power, reach for the stars, and live each day as if it was their last. Such generic and impersonal slogans—plastered on posters, stickers, and other marketable items—do not inspire me much. When Jennifer told me "I believe in you," she was looking at *me* straight in the eyes and spoke those words with a conviction that reached me inside.

A core member who enjoys community gatherings and welcoming people, Jennifer is often convivial, bringing humor, laughter, and outspokenness to social occasions. But this time, when she said and repeated those four words, I - believe - in - you, she spoke in a tone that was almost solemn. The hug she later gave me was an affectionate demonstration of her powerful words, which were as simple as they were deep. Do I—do we—believe in ourselves? What does believing in ourselves mean?

To believe means "to trust." The Greek word for belief, *pisteuo*, means to have confidence. In this book, I therefore use believing and trusting interchangeably. Its two sections, "Believing in Yourself" and "Believing in the Other," are inter-related as both are an invitation to trust, but each has a different emphasis.

In the first part of the book, "Believing in Yourself," I hope you can hear Jennifer's words—"I believe in you"—and make them your own: "I believe in myself." Believing—or trusting—in ourselves is an interior attitude, a personal orientation. It is not about achieving something, but about receiving the gift of our being. When we trust someone else we let go and have confidence in the other. In the same way, when we trust ourselves, we can have confidence in our being without having to master it. Shaping our lives is surely important, but if we try to shape our lives without trusting our innate value as unique human beings, the actions we might undertake to become a certain kind of person, the words we might use to define ourselves, or the belief we might hold to give meaning to what we live, can risk moving us away from who we are.

Fundamentally, believing in ourselves does not merely mean relying on our capabilities, our abilities and our willpower, as if we have to control life; it implies embracing our beauty and value, accepting ourselves, as well as trusting our deep desires beyond our fears. I hope that what you will find here will help you with this.

We will first tackle the question "Who are we?" and shed light on the importance of our being. We will then explore the importance of loving ourselves and reconciling with our histories, which might have given us conflictual understandings of who we are. We will then touch on embracing our abilities and inabilities (acknowledging our gifts but also our human limits), the importance of listening to our embodied selves, and the courage to claim our voice.

The second part of the book, "Believing in the Other," builds on the first, but the focus shifts from ourselves onto others so as to attend to the relationships between ourselves and them: we will explore ways in which we can let others know that we believe in them. First, we will reflect on what it means to encounter the other and to be with them. We will then focus on trusting the other at the margins of our reality, beyond the walls that get created around ourselves and groups. Lastly, we will affirm the importance of affirming, forgiving, and celebrating the other.

Believing in ourselves and others is not so much an intellectual endeavor, but an experience that touches our whole being. It is a matter of the heart, where all our faculties converge. The approach in these pages will therefore be holistic, considering the various dimensions—or better, the oneness—of our being.

Believing in Yourself

Who Are We?

Believing in ourselves can manifest itself at any moment, as when we make a decision, trust our fundamental desires and needs, or speak authentic words. However, such belief also gets nourished and grows day after day as we let go of the masks, fears, and anxieties that can hinder our authentic self from flourishing. Although we may know many things about ourselves—our physical features, histories, ways of expression and beliefs—who we are is also a profound mystery. There is so much about ourselves that we don't know! As we grow in self-belief, we become more comfortable with the knowns and unknowns of our lives. We trust that our unique being develops through what we are aware of, and also what we are not aware of.

At L'Arche there are many events that community members and guests attend where they can meet people, connect, and have a shared communal experience. These events include people introducing themselves to others. As I led quite a few of these events, I sought to facilitate those self-introductions by encouraging attendees to sit in a circle and introduce themselves one by one. As it is valuable to get to know who is who, all were invited to mention their name and where they lived or came from. In listening to people, I attended to how they presented themselves—their words, their tone of voice, their body language—and how they introduced themselves.

In introducing themselves to others during community gatherings, some speak out their names with audible strength, as if they have no fear letting their presence be known, while others do so more timidly, as if they are uncomfortable being at the center of attention. Most mention where they come from, be it their home or the geographical location they traveled from, identifying a sense of connection to something besides themselves; but some don't mention it, possibly because they simply may not want to or because they may not feel a strong sense of connection to a specific place. During these introductions, Jennifer always prefers introducing herself after everyone else; besides mentioning her name, she talks about other topics, including the rights of people with disabilities, facts about her family members, and the background of L'Arche, leaving some people confused as to who she is introducing. Another core member, Karen, does not talk at all but looks down or turns to the side as soon as it is her turn to present herself. She remains silent, mentioning nothing, as if fear holds her from claiming and voicing her name in front of so many people.

Yet this analysis of how people introduce themselves could also be reversed and re-written with a different emphasis to give us another understanding of how they choose to present who they are. We can frame it this way: some speak out their names with vocal strength, as if not allowing for a quiet questioning of who they are, whereas others mention their name more timidly, testing the waters of the mystery they are. Most guests mention where they come from, as if they have only one location to identify with, whereas others don't, as if they feel that they belong to a broader space without physical boundaries. During these introductions, Jennifer mentions her name and talks about disability rights, her family and the background of L'Arche, as if her story is deeply tied to that of other people and to her identity as a member of various communities. Karen, on the other hand, looks down when her turn for introducing herself arrives and remains silent, as if resisting the pressure to identify herself quickly and openly in front of so many people.

Our sense of who we are is a multi-layered reality that can be understood in various ways. Any simplistic "one-size-fits-all" answer would not do it justice. We get a sense of identity from the life elements that we inhabit—our names, our relationships, our environments, our beliefs, and so on. Yet our selfhood goes well beyond these. We can use words to describe ourselves, while there is much more about which we are not even aware and that remains unspoken.

I cannot give a final or complete answer to the "who we are" question, not only because it is well beyond my scope, but also because there really isn't one exhaustive answer. For thousands of years lovers, thinkers, philosophers, researchers, artists—and presumably mostly everyone else—have tried to answer the identity question through their suppositions, possibilities, arguments, guesses, analyses, and imaginings.

Our physical selves present the biological fruit of our parents' relationship. Our eyes might contain a spark of our spirits, be they downcast or joyful. As we age, we might reflect on our histories and how they have influenced our perception of selfhood—the people we have encountered on our paths, the places we have been, and the moments we have lived through. As we ponder the experiences that have formed our perception of life, we might be grateful for loving relationships and feel upset by encounters with people that have left us feeling alone or alienated.

When we introduce ourselves to others, we usually mention our names and let the conversation shift to how we are doing at that moment or what we are involved with in life. We easily come up with a list of our likes and dislikes to provide others an idea of what interests us and what doesn't. If needed, we can summarize a bit of our personal history, so as to give a sense of our background. In more professional settings, we might even provide an informal list of our activities and skills, to illustrate the work of our minds and of our hands.

Whatever we think or sense about ourselves and share with others, however, is always limited. Although having an experiential sense and knowing factual information about ourselves gives us an identity idea, we ultimately are a mystery to ourselves. This lack of knowing does not mean that we are merely big question marks moving around, as if we couldn't know anything about ourselves; it means that when we confront the essential questions of our lives (who are we, why are we here, and where are we going) it is not so obvious to have definite answers. Even humanistic and spiritual answers do not satisfy our questions—and sometimes our doubts—about the meaning of our lives. We might have a heart-felt intuition, a logical argument, a firm or fickle hope, or a faith-based creed that give a sense of personal meaning to our being, but this does not erase our human condition that for millennia has sought a fuller understanding of it.

How to believe in ourselves, then, when we don't even fully know ourselves? Thinking and intellectualizing about our identity won't necessarily do, as filtering it through the conceptualizations of our minds can be both helpful and confusing. Processing the many thoughts, emotions, beliefs, inputs, and unresolved conflicts that cross our minds requires great mental energy and can produce a chaotic understanding of our identity. Focusing on how we feel about ourselves can also be limiting. Our emotional lives are constantly alternating and many factors, from the mood we wake up with to big events that shake us up, can influence them. What we feel one day may differ from what we feel the day after; even within the same day we may experience a roller-coaster of emotions.

If what we think and what we feel about ourselves do not give us the full picture of who we are, however, we can still be in touch with a deeper level beneath our thoughts and emotions that does not depend on their unpredictability. This deeper level remains within us throughout our history, the experiences we go through, and the changes that happen to us. It can be a grounding experience of awareness: "I am."

Sometimes a distinction is made between the authentic (or true) self and the false self. Although the distinction sounds too black and white, the authentic self denotes living in tune with our deepest level, while the false self is the facade or mask behind which, for whatever reason, we may hide.

Karen exhibits this tension between being authentic and putting on masks. Soon approaching old age, before coming to community Karen used to live in one of the dehumanizing institutions to which for most of the twentieth century large numbers of people with intellectual disabilities were marginalized. In those dismal institutional conditions she was badly treated and became aggressive, beginning to act like an animal to protect herself, to the point of making barking sounds and biting to defend her territory. In community, however, we have tried to reveal to her that she is precious and cherished as she is. Through living in a welcoming home with a few other people, Karen has exhibited great gifts of nurturing and welcome. She cares for the people around her, and often invites them to watch television shows by her side. She also likes to show concern for the neighborhood pets.

Community has given Karen a space for her authentic, considerate side to flourish, even if at times the past re-surfaces within her as do the animal-like behaviors. Sometimes, when she seems stressed, she can bite people. At other times she goes out wearing a big brown plastic hairy lion mask to hide in. Around Karen a group of people, including friends who often share time with her, support her and try to look beyond these external behaviors. They help her communicate her inner state without resorting to masks and aggression. When she speaks of being an animal, we try to affirm that she is a great lady. When she presents herself as a lion caring for her "pride," I respond that she is a woman who cares about her friends, shifting the conversation from the illusion of the mask to her authentic self.

Although most of us do not go around wearing lion masks, we often do wear inner masks. These masks allow us to hide and present a false image of ourselves. The more we wear these masks, the easier it becomes to believe in them and identify with them, even if they don't reflect who we are deep inside. Our masks are probably not plastic Halloween-style creations we place over our heads. More likely they consist of inner dynamics and mechanisms that may be the product of years of pressures we have put on ourselves to match our own idealized self-image or to be how others want us to be, insofar as these distanced us from our own reality. Our masks may be the result of habits, patterns, and roles we created for ourselves as our fears and insecurities came up against threats from the external world. They may be ways of thinking or acting that we learned from others but that never really fit us, or that were helpful at some point but that do not fit us anymore.

As social beings we have learned many of our living patterns from others. In one way, this has saved our lives. As children and youngsters, for example, we survived by learning from parents or teachers what foods are edible and what is dangerous, or when to cross a street and when not to. In more subtle ways, through their advice, opinions, and feedback, the people close to us might have helped us recognize and claim places within ourselves where we might have been hesitant to venture on our own. Think about friends listening, challenging, and inspiring us to listen to our interior needs and take the risk of following our deepest aspirations. All this positive social learning, which has helped us grow in our selfhood (and still does), can be kept, appreciated, and shared. From the people surrounding us, however, we have also learned living patterns that may have alienated us from our authentic selves and that we therefore need to "unlearn" or leave aside.

How can Karen see that her mask might not serve her well anymore (if it ever did) and that now in her community she is loved and respected, to the point that she can freely speak her name and show her face without hiding behind an aggressive lion face? There are many moments in home life when she is unafraid to be herself and to claim who she is—she is a strong, outspoken, and determined lady! Yet, sometimes, she goes back to wearing the mask. We ourselves, like her, might experience moments when we feel free to be who we are but also moments when we go back to wearing masks, often without even realizing it. For many, taking away all the masks at once might be uncalled for, as they may be so used to them that not wearing one can make them feel unsafe and in deep anguish. It might take time to let go of the masks and grow rooted in one's authentic self.

Putting on masks, pretending to be someone we are not and avoiding our own truths, takes impressive energy and can be quite alienating. Letting our authentic self be free, instead, can feel life-giving and harmonious, in tune with our nature, without needing to do ourselves any violence. Imagine the development of an oak, which grows from an acorn symbolism. Before becoming such a majestic tree, the acorn must send roots into the ground to anchor the plant and seek water, surviving the different seasons. As this process unfolds, the acorn does what is in its deepest nature to do. It does not try to be something else, does not compare itself to others, and does not worry about what it should be doing. Within the acorn the laws of nature just happen, resulting in an abundance of life as it becomes a tree. Psychologist Raffaele Morelli uses the acorn symbolism to illustrate how it is not the control of ourselves nor the pressure to be someone that frees us to be who we are; what helps us flourish is the simplicity of letting our being be and develop according to its inner life, without pursuing false identities.[2]

Over its lengthy lifespan an oak tree experiences changes: it can grow to the height of a fifteen-story building, can produce as many as ten million acorns, with its leaves changing color and falling as the seasons unfold. Fundamentally, however, even through so many changes, it remains an oak. In a similar way, we too change and are influenced by various factors as we develop, but these transformations can bring us closer to our authentic selves or at least need not pull us away from "the 'you' and 'me' that exist consistently through all the physical, emotional, mental, and external changes we have experienced,"[3] as Ken Sedlak describes.

Believing in ourselves means freeing our authentic selves as we lower the masks that constrain us into roles that don't fit. This is not a mere intellectual task or emotional process, but something that emerges from deep within. We may not fully know who we are—we are a mystery onto ourselves!—and our feelings towards ourselves can change, but we can be confident that our own selves can emerge spontaneously, if we let it happen. Our beings, after all, naturally want to be free. No wonder Karen, after wearing her lion mask for a while, in the end always decides to take it off and set it aside.

Being Ourselves

To trust ourselves we need to give ourselves permission to just be, breathing freely with the confidence that who we are is enough. There is no mechanical way to produce this. It just happens, like breathing just happens. Allow yourself to breathe. It is not an effort we have to master or an activity to add to our schedule; it is about trusting in the life that emerges from deep within our being.

I'd like to introduce core member Ted, who seems content with just...being. Ted, a humble man with Down syndrome, is very communicative. Being non-verbal, he expresses himself mainly through sounds, facial expressions, and hand gestures. Whether happy or upset, Ted's glances and sounds tend to reveal his state and emotions. Whether he wants to do something or not, he communicates through gestures.

When we were housemates Ted consistently sought and asked for one thing: coffee. Throughout the day, at various moments, in different contexts, and with different people, his hands would gesture for coffee, accompanied by a gentle whisper that said "hy," as in happy. This was the nickname he used for his drink of choice, which he repeated various times, "hy hy hy" ("coffee coffee coffee"). Coffee did indeed seem to bring gladness, or even solace, to Ted, who enjoyed sitting on a couch or on a chair, at home or in a coffeehouse, slowly sipping from his cup. At times the coffee would burn his lips, so he would utter, "Way warm!" Most of Ted's words revolved around the coffee experience, a pleasant and quiet happening. Undoubtedly, the one appliance thoroughly used at the community home was the coffee maker, on which Ted kept a close eye. One afternoon, Ted exited the kitchen carrying three cups of coffee—one in each hand and the third one held in the crook of his arm! Good thing decaf was an option.

On weekdays Ted worked at a day program. He still made sure that his coffee times were respected, however. On weekends, after church on Sunday mornings, a community outing for coffee and donuts at a local cafe was an event that Ted never missed. Ted's coffee sipping was never out of season. It was not just a culinary fancy of his; it was a ritual of being. Ted could sit for a long time by his cup, not doing much. Although without it Ted was still able to be present and aware, often sitting in the living room gazing and looking around, whether at home relaxing or working, the coffee cup seemed to be a centering experience for him. After all, if some people use bells or humming sounds to center themselves, why can't a coffee cup do?

Our society is obsessed with doing. A person is often valued in terms of activity and productivity. This leaves people with disabilities consistently at the tail end of the social scale. The emphasis on doing can also create or awaken compulsive and workaholic tendencies, with the consequences these imply. Some people even speak about their busyness with a strange tone of masochistic satisfaction. Giving more importance to being than doing is essential for our well-being, and for society's. We are who we are, not what we do or what we produce. If we want to trust our being, we would do well to let go of performance anxiety. For example, as you read these words I'd invite you not to worry about finishing the chapter and encourage you to put the book down, your eyes open or closed, breathing in and breathing out, aware of your breathing, returning to the book afterwards. You are present in the moment, you just are.

In daily life, one way to savor the primacy of being over doing, even amid what may be a busy schedule, is to treat leisure as a priority, just as a relaxed coffee-time is a priority for Ted. Coming from Italy, I am familiar with and enjoy *il dolce far niente*, the sweet doing nothing. Whether walking around the city streets, strolling around a piazza, sitting at a cafe', resting, meeting up with pals to talk about everything and nothing, or taking periodic times of rest and renewal, there is a pace in Italian life that respects the importance of leisure.

Leisure, however, is not confined to one culture; it is available everywhere, as it is a quality of how we are in the world. Ted knows about it! Culturally, it is not a new concept either. In ancient times, the Greeks and the Romans gave importance to leisurely, contemplative time. Both Jewish and Christian traditions, grounded in the Biblical story of God resting on the last day of creation, highlight the importance of keeping a day of rest. For Jews, the Sabbath is a reminder of God freeing his people from slavery; for Christians it is a celebration of Christ's rising and rescuing humanity from death. In both traditions, the emphasis of this leisurely day is not on our doing and our efforts, but on the freedom God brings and reveals.

In my own experience, the moments of leisure I shared with Ted and with other friends imply a restful "being with." These moments can also include sharing an activity, but I enter those moments without expectations, as these are not moments for achieving something. I also enjoy leisure time alone, as I am present to myself in the moment and feel what I feel, as I contemplate reality, as I listen to music, as I eat, and sometimes as I take an afternoon siesta.

Every person has their own way of tapping into leisure. Henry David Thoreau describes walking in the outdoors: "When I go out of the house for a walk, uncertain as yet whither I will bend my steps, and submit myself to my instinct to decide for me, I find, strange and whimsical as it may seem, that I finally and inevitably settle southwest, toward some particular wood or meadow or deserted pasture or hill in that direction."[4] His words convey a letting go: his instincts navigate him through nature and his self knows where to go. He doesn't control his being, he follows it. He is not planning his steps, nor expecting to find something specific, but somewhere he is being led. Cecile Andrews, on the other hand, recalls a half hour of leisure watching her sheets dry out on a sunny Seattle day: "The sun was out, but it wasn't really hot; there was a mild breeze that gently billowed out my sheets. I realized, after about a half-hour had passed, that I had spent the whole time literally watching my sheets dry. Maybe there's something to the old cliché, as exciting as watching grass grow. In a state of pure leisure, watching sheets dry can be rapturous."[5] She was so present in the moment that even sheets drying could be enchanting.

Philosopher Joseph Pieper associates leisure with the "surge of new life that flows out to us when we give ourselves to the contemplation of a blossoming rose, a sleeping child, or of a divine mystery."[6] Such an attitude, he believed, is not "of the one who intervenes but of the one who opens himself; not of someone who seizes but of one who lets go, who lets himself go."[7] Pieper wrote *Leisure, the Basis of Culture* amid the post-World War II rebuilding of Germany, emphasizing the importance of taking leisure seriously so as to understand the reasons for building. The "sweet doing nothing" of leisure helps us recognize what is important to our beings, and therefore affects and re-orients our direction, helping keep it humane. When I drove Ted to the local coffee house to sit down and quietly sip coffee together, it was apparent how he enjoyed this moment of leisure and found it important, so much so that he ensured that such moments happened frequently, almost to the point of structuring his days around coffee time. Human priorities can be so simple and delightful.

Through the years, I have accompanied many assistants as they begin their journeys in community. These assistants mostly came after schooling (high school or college) to work or volunteer in our homes. I have been privileged to hear their stories and support them through their joys and struggles as they adjusted to life with their new housemates with and without disabilities. More than once I have noticed how some were so focused on staying active that they didn't quite know what to do with themselves on their two weekly rest days of "time away." Even when they were working in the homes, they still doubted whether they were doing enough—supporting people enough, helping around the house enough, working well enough—and wondered how they could fill the time more—finding new activities, coming up with new plans, looking ahead for new opportunities. I heard their concerns and listened to their mental processing. They spoke from a place of anxiety, the product of an age that asks people to always push for more. Not surprisingly, this anxiousness went hand in hand with a tendency towards perfectionism, which is both a cause of and a common response to anxiety. As I witnessed their inner agitation, I usually tried to highlight the gift of their presence to community and encouraged them not to over-fill their schedules with things but remain present to themselves and to others, even if this meant sitting quietly in the living room or going on a walk with someone. I encouraged them to notice how in their shared life alongside people with disabilities they were being invited to let go of the rush to achieve more and more (and potentially experiencing burn-out at some point), and to enter into the realm of being-with, where leisure can take the form of watching a movie together for the twentieth time, going to a nearby park to read a book on the changing seasons, or staying at the dinner table after the meal to chat about animals, pop-stars, and funny noises.

Each month, the assistants from the different homes gather to reflect on their experiences in community and learn from them, a meeting called "formation." Different from training mostly focused on building skills, which surely has its own important place, formation focuses primarily on merging experience and reflection, and so, it is hoped, leading to wisdom. In leading formation, I put together a program for the assistants to help them reflect on relevant themes and issues. During an April formation, held between Easter events and a Seder dinner, I sensed that the assistants were feeling a bit busy with all the preparations and hosting of the season. We began our time together by going around the circle to check in on how each one was doing, and we had a moment of reflection on how hard and yet important it is to leave empty space in our lives, even if this meant sitting down and doing nothing for ten minutes. I wanted the main part of the formation, however, to move beyond talking about this and actually trying it. I therefore asked everyone to remain sitting in the quiet for ten minutes, without doing anything. I mentioned I would let them know when the ten minutes were over so that they didn't need to worry about keeping an eye on the time. As we entered this time of silence, some closed their eyes, some kept them open. In the background we could hear the ticking of a clock on the wall, cars passing by on the street in front the house, and light chair sounds if people slightly moved on them. Reflecting back on this "non-activity," not only did the time go by faster than I thought (even too fast!) but it was easier—and even more enjoyable—just to sit in the quiet for ten minutes as a group than I had initially imagined. Upon announcing that the ten minutes were over I added that our time together in formation was actually finished for the day—we had come together to do nothing. One of the assistants had written to me that morning asking if he could skip the formation so that he could have more time to cook the chicken for the evening meal. I encouraged him to come, not because I took pleasure in adding one more thing to his schedule (to the contrary), but because if he was so busy that he could not attend our monthly meeting then he truly needed those ten minutes of empty space.

It would be extreme, however, to think that we can let ourselves be only by doing nothing and leaving empty space. Life in community—life in general!—can be eventful and often feels occupied, down to a very concrete and practical level. We live in the world, and there are appointments to fulfill, meals to make, various needs to cater to, jobs to do and commitments to schedule. Throughout all these tasks, however, we can ensure that we don't disperse ourselves but let ourselves be present in the action, so what we do is the fruit of our being and not of our scattering. The care with which we cook a meal, the attention we put into creating something for others as we perform our jobs, the ways we move from one activity to another throughout the day, can all allow us to convey and express who we are. If, on the other hand, our actions come and go anxiously they will likely precisely convey that … anxiety.

One evening, assistant Jacques was making dinner for about thirty people gathered at the community home for a special event. Earlier in the day he shared with the assistants' team how concerned he was about this dinner. Was he going to make enough food? Was the recipe going to be good? Would there be enough time for the cooking? His face seemed lost in worry. At a certain point, as his apprehension over the meal built, I mentioned how he could leave the cooking to someone else, which could have been me, rather than going through the process with such anxiety. I didn't necessarily expect him to delegate the cooking, but I wanted to make a simple point. If cooking the meal stressed him out with the many "what ifs" that could go wrong, serving the meal with anxious hands would have affected people with that anxiety and would have clashed with the spirit of the celebration. If, instead, he allowed himself to be present in the action of cooking, rather than hopping from one worry to the next, then the work of his hands could have had a different quality.

If we want to trust ourselves we are invited to surrender to our being, remaining present to it, confident that deep within we can have a sense of where we need to be and how we need to act, whether this means sitting down at a coffeehouse or making dinner for thirty people.

Loving Ourselves

When we love ourselves, we can more easily let ourselves be. If we don't like who we are, if we don't believe we are precious, we will be mired in insecurity and distrust, moving through life cautiously and fearfully. If we love ourselves, on the other hand, we grow comfortable in living out and enjoying our uniqueness, claiming the freedom to be who we are.

You may have met people that you sensed were free within, comfortable in their own skin and not afraid to be different from others. For me, one of these people is Mark, a friendly and peace-making man who has an intellectual disability. A gentle soul, Mark is a genuinely loving person, quick to embrace people and to say "I am sorry" if he thinks he has done something wrong. If there is tension among his friends, Mark tries to bring a word of comfort and care, often accompanied by a warm smile. His hearing is impaired, as well as his capacity to verbalize what he wants to say. His broken speech can be hard to understand, even if he patiently repeats himself when asked. Mark often talks to himself, sometimes loudly, even into the evening hours. It seems as if he re-lives past events in his mind, vocalizing them as if they are happening again in the present, to the point of giving voice to the different people involved in the imagined scene.

Mark and I lived in community together, albeit in two different homes. We would see each other almost every weekend at the community gym outing. Going to the gym right after dinner on a Friday night wasn't everyone's favorite weekly activity—for sure it wasn't for me—but about fifteen community members gathered there each week to exercise and stay healthy. Some exercised on the stationary bikes, a few ventured onto the weight machines, some played with the oversized stability balls in the vacant fitness room. Week after week Mark's gym routine consisted in heading to the fitness room as well, but to mainly sit on its wooden floor and stay there throughout the gym outing. From his floor seat, Mark would look around and talk to himself, his eyes moving left to right, staring into space. He had a good appetite and exercise would have benefited him, but he preferred to voyage in his mind without touching any machines. As assistants, we respected Mark's unique gym routine, and at times passed around a plastic ball to engage him in some movement, even if he made that last quite briefly. Sometimes I sat next to Mark, to be present to him and keep him company. As I looked at him, I noticed his facial expressions change as if he was watching a movie in his mind, and I heard the alternating voice pitches he would make while talking to himself, as he smiled looking upward.

Mark is a human being who is very much himself—free to give voice to whatever goes through his mind, free to embrace people as they are, free to ask for forgiveness, free to let his boundaries be known, free to go to a gym and stay seated on the floor for close to an hour. Although society's questionable notion of normalcy would deem Mark an outsider, he might be freer to be himself than many who follow standardized rules without question. After all, in "normal" society, people are encouraged to be and act in certain ways, at times to the point of becoming very much like each other. This tyranny of the norm, to use a term employed by the author Lennard J. Davis,[8] is not always overt, but imposed through hidden powers—from expectations of what an independent self-made citizen should be to media images of what a good-looking successful person should appear like. Mark, however, does not seem to care about these influences. He is who he is. Recalling Mark's "out of the box" manner, how can I forget when he and I, alongside two other community members, went on a trip to visit the New York City area and Mark took a cowboy hat with him for the wearing—a culturally interesting and highly original move for that city context.

Mark had a unique connection with one person—his dad, who passed away years ago and who was, from stories, told, very proud of his son. A fire chief, he introduced Mark to the world of fire trucks, helmets, and teamship. Even after his father's passing, whenever Mark visits the fire-department he worked at, firefighters and firehouse staff welcome him with open arms and a celebratory spirit, as if he is a super-star. Mark even joins in their city parade each year.

Although I never met Mark's dad and only heard of their loving relationship, I have witnessed to how loved Mark is by the community around him. I can say that he is cherished, treated with respect and care. I wouldn't be surprised if this legacy of love has empowered him to be comfortable to live in his unique way, with the courage to be as he is without worrying about measuring up to an average standard.

Besides the love he receives from others, I also sense that Mark loves himself in such a way that he is fine being himself. I have never heard him express concern about comparing himself to others nor does he seem worried about what they might think of him. He is as authentic with himself as he is with fellow human beings, letting his thoughts, voices, and feelings emerge and flow out of him, without spending a lot of energy on "bottling them in." His personality is out in the open. Although his intellectual disability might preclude his having certain worries that the general population might be subject to, explaining his freedom of spirit by focusing on his disability would be reductive and neglectful of his complexity as a human being. I have known core members who have come to community from unloving experiences and hard pasts that even after many years are still affected and limited by them, their anguish influencing their way of being in the world and coloring how they relate to reality. I have not witnessed such a disposition in Mark.

Love does free us to be our authentic selves, but I also realize the danger of saying such a beautiful and over-used word: love. The term has been spoken in so many ways that declaring "love is the answer," as truthful as it is, can awaken within our imagination little heart figures and red-shaded greetings cards. Nonetheless, if we give up the stereotypes and think about our own life experience, we might realize how love makes the difference between life and death.

Although each of us has experienced life-giving love in ways that are unique to our individual stories, we can find loving instances and moments that most can connect with. For instance, during infancy love sustained our being. When we were babies we relied completely on our parental figures for sustenance, care, and protection. If we were not washed, clothed, and kept warm, we could have gotten sick; if we were not fed, we would have perished. Love kept us alive.

Growing up, love continued to sustain our lives. We might have felt encouraged by a friend's hand on our shoulder during a difficult moment or we might have felt relieved by finding a listening ear when we needed to process things. We might still remember the time someone looked at us and revealed to us how valued we were, or we might be grateful to those ancestors that have provided a better life for us than they had. We might have felt excited and lightened up as we began dating and discovered the fervor of romance; we may still be enjoying the fruits of enduring commitment to a special someone.

During my time in community, I would occasionally visit Aurelie, a close friend with whom I'd share a weekend home-cooked lunch. No matter how things in my personal and community life were going, at her house I could chat and relax. Aurelie was middle-aged but still single and was losing hope of finding a man with whom to have a romantic relationship. Her outlook was dim, her humor slightly cynical, and her mood weighed down. In past relationships she seemed insecure—unsure of her partners' feelings towards her, confused about some of their behaviors and unclear about their motives. Her doubts, disappointments, and low self-esteem restrained her spirit. At one point, however, she began dating a man she met through a friend. I knew right away that this relationship was different from the others. As the two continued going out and exploring their relationship, I noticed that her eyes carried a new hope, that her mood felt lighter and her words contained a softer quality. Aurelie was still Aurelie, yet in encountering love she was freed to be herself in a new way as the blockages, walls, and fears that had restrained her started falling down.

As I write about the liberating power of love, I'd like to avoid speaking of love only as an idyllic reality. Alvin and Gloria, who have intellectual disabilities, have been married for quite some time now. They live in their own apartment within community, with external assistants visiting and supporting them as needed. The two share a special bond, as well as a sense of humor. One time when I invited them to share a meal with me, I noticed right away how they often teased each other, followed by a glance or smile of comradery. Their irony was typical of partners that have been together for many years, loving each other and in some way "putting up" with each other, living an enduring commitment through exciting moments and difficult ones.

The love between friends can see different seasons too. Core members Jacob and Louis are housemates that have lived together for over ten years. Periodically, Louis says irritating things to Jacob, who responds with a serious and severe look. When this happens the atmosphere in the house tenses up: the two are waging a psychological battle with each other and everyone around them picks up on it. After a few minutes, days, or weeks, peace is always reached, over and over again, with Louis tickling Jacob (who gets a lot of laughter out of it) and Jacob reminding him that they are still friends after all. Their relationship has seen various cycles—and it has not always been easy. Jacob and Louis irritate each other and make peace, irritate each other and make peace, on and on. We might connect to such a relationship as we think of any person in our lives we love and with whom we have had moments of closeness as well as moments of distance, experiences of delight as well as experiences of suffering. Love is a journey of growth, with joy and sorrow co-existing next to each other.

As we continue reflecting on our experiences of love in its different forms, whether with family, friends or partners, we likely see that people have generally neither been completely loving nor totally unloving towards us, as if we lived in black and white extremes. If our parents protected and nurtured us, they might also have hurt us or neglected us. If our friends were there when we needed them, they might also have disappointed us when they didn't understand us or were absent at an important moment in our lives. If our partners cherished and affirmed us, they might also have betrayed us and behaved in ways that sent us down a spiral of depression. No human being can love perfectly. On our earthly journey, experiences of love are often accompanied by contrasting realities, as people hold within themselves a variety of emotions, tendencies, and needs.

We can receive all the goodness that others' love gives us, but also recognize when people do not really love us. Although it is important to receive love from others, it is risky and eventually unhealthy to base ourselves on that, as if our identity and freedom depended on it, ready to fluctuate and ultimately fall apart whenever that love diminishes or is taken away. We can, however, commit to loving ourselves and let this profoundly influence our lives. Although others can help us experience love, if we don't love ourselves in the first place, we will live unsettled lives—waiting for others to give us what we neglect to give ourselves.

Loving ourselves implies treating ourselves with the same gentleness, understanding, empathy, and encouragement that we'd like to be treated with or with which we'd treat someone we care about. As we love ourselves, we appreciate and celebrate who we are—not wanting to be anyone else. You may have heard people describe their relationship with another in terms such as, "She is my best friend, she just gets me and is always there when I need her" or, "When I met that man I knew he was the one I wanted to be with." What if we gifted ourselves with similar loving affirmations and find they positively influence how we treat ourselves — enjoying our presence, claiming our beauty and liking it, giving space to our potential, giving ourselves the attention, time, and care we need, listening to what we have to say and cherishing our voice. In other words, claiming our belovedness.

It might sound strange to think of being the beloved... of ourselves! Isn't someone usually the "beloved" of someone else? Yet if we are not our own beloved ones, the love we give others or would like to receive in return can easily become a way to mask our insecurity and self-alienation. In any type of relationship or community there is a real danger of focusing on loving others while forgetting to love oneself. I have often met people who appear considerate and patient with others, while being frustrated and rigid with their own selves. Sometimes they might cloak this behavior with psychological or religious language, using assertions like, "I should not be self-centered" (as if loving oneself meant being obsessed with oneself), or "I am here to serve others" (as if loving others somehow meant not loving self). By these ideological copouts, they end up neglecting themselves to the point of treating their person as a nobody, which is neither psychologically sound nor spiritually healthy.

The "golden rule"—treating others as you'd want to be treated—is a consistent principle across various philosophical, religious, and narrative traditions. In the Buddhist tradition this takes the form of a question: "For a state that is not pleasant or delightful to me must also be to him also; and a state that is not pleasing or delightful to me, how could I inflict that upon another?" (Samyutta Nikaya V, 535.53-354.2). In Islamic writings, the thirteenth saying of Al-Nawawi's Forty Hadith spells out: "None of you [truly] believes until he loves for his brother that which he loves for himself." The ancient Indian Mahābhārata states that there is a "sum of duty: do not do to others what would cause pain if done to you" (5:1517). The gospel call to "love your neighbor as yourself" (Mk 12:31) is also mentioned within the Torah: "You shall not take vengeance or bear a grudge against any of your people, but you shall love your neighbor as yourself" (Lev 19:18). Although the universal teaching of lovingly treating others as yourself is well-known, that last part of it— "as yourself"—is too easily forgotten or overlooked, even if it is crucial in understanding healthy love. Carl Jung once hinted at this when he wrote,

"That I feed the hungry, that I forgive an insult, that I love my enemy in the name of Christ—all these are undoubtedly great virtues. What I do unto the least of my brethren, that I do unto Christ. But what if I should discover that the least amongst them all, the poorest of all the beggars, the most impudent of all the offenders, the very enemy himself—that these are within me, and that I myself stand in need of the alms of my own kindness—that I myself am the enemy that must be loved—what then?"[9]

We can grow in love towards self, but such an experience is also deeply connected to the stance of "just being" explored in the previous chapter. Love can involve initiative on our part if we want to cultivate it, but it also "just happens." In relationships, for example, love appears spontaneously when we sense a connection, interest or attraction towards someone, but also involves making choices and acting in certain ways if we are committed to that person, including when challenges arise, whichever kind of love we share with them (familial, love of friendship or romantic love). Love therefore asks for a commitment to others—and to ourselves—that involves initiative and decision-making. Fundamentally, however, it flows out of us. Daniel J O'Hanlon, S.J., writes, "It is possible to allow love to simply emerge out of awareness; without making its cultivation the first object of concern. ... This practice seems to spring out of the conviction that love and compassion are the natural movement of our true self."[10]

Trusting in ourselves is the foundation for loving ourselves. We trust those we love, not those we want to run away from. When we don't love ourselves, we easily run away from our center into clingy relationships with other people, unconsciously using them to satisfy our frustrated needs and fill our inner void under the guise of love. We nervously compare ourselves to those around us, depending on them for our self-worth, and become overly concerned with how others might see us, becoming paralyzed by our insecurities. When we love ourselves, instead, we grow rooted in our being, cherishing and living it out.

Claiming a Deeper Love

As with the love we receive from others, the love we have for ourselves can wither or be mixed with disappointments, insecurities, self-judgement, and self-hate. It can easily fluctuate. There is a deep level within each of us, however, where we are in unity with a love larger and more consistent than ours, and which may be considered the ground of our being.

Jennifer, the core member I introduced earlier, is a woman who, similarly to Mark, is not afraid to be herself. Jennifer unapologetically asserts her presence the moment she enters a room. She might greet each person around her with a hug, burst out into loud laughter in a quiet space over something that gives her joy, or share her personal life in a flow-of-consciousness style with people she never met before. As merrily confident as she is in herself, however, Jennifer is also distressed by negative thoughts or voices she experiences in her head. It is not clear if these are mere thoughts or actual voices, but they articulate mean and scary things to her, bringing her to question her worth.

Jennifer's upsetting thoughts understandably turn her mood somber, even dark. These thoughts sometimes lead her to shout and cry. This can be so unsettling that, when it happens at home, other core members move to another area of the house and the assistants are left wondering as to how to support her. This tense energy can be so strong that Jennifer gets angry at herself for what she cannot control. The anger and self-accusation can be so powerful that screaming and crying are her—understandable—responses. In some way she reminds me of another core member, Delilah, who reacts similarly, but more violently, to strong feelings arising within her, hitting herself on the head in self-deprecation.

Despite her changeable thoughts and mood cycles, Jennifer seems to find solace in her spirituality and faith tradition. She serves as a cantor at her local church, joyfully partakes in religious celebrations, and when it is time to say goodnight, she channels peace as she blesses assistants by placing a hand on their foreheads. She manifests her spirituality not only by these actions, but also in a favorite hobby, producing artwork. On her eclectic art pieces, Jennifer likes to draw heart symbols, crosses, coffee cups, peace signs, and lit candles surrounded by smiling suns and sleeping stars. These welcoming, hopeful symbols she draws convey a peace-loving and hospitable spirit. When she comes home after work, Jennifer finds rest in filling the shapes and patterns in her mandala coloring books with different shades.

Even if she sometimes experiences scary thoughts and fluctuating moods, Jennifer always remembers how to enter the peace and quiet of her artistic inspiration, touching a deeper level of her being where she can feel more at ease. No matter how loud her thoughts might scream at her or how low her mood can get she knows how to return to those warm and welcoming artistic spaces. It can be a true discipline to return to spaces of calm and keep faithful to them, tasting a peace that transcends the day-to-day ups and downs that otherwise might darken a whole day.

We may know well the power of negative thinking, of self-deprecation or self-accusation. Although we might not scream in frustration like Jennifer nor hit ourselves like Delilah, we might be doing so within. Agreeing with those dark thoughts of self-judgment, becoming our own harsh critics, believing the voice of despair, and giving reign to low self-esteem, are just some of the ways by which we might get upset and punish ourselves. By agreeing with or even nervously fighting with those annoying little voices we can threaten our peace.

Dark inner voices—whether they whisper or shout—need not have ultimate power over us. No matter what we might be experiencing on the surface, as we move within, towards the center of our being, we can reach a space of unconditional, reliable, and eternal love. This space goes by many names, but it is often called inner center or heart. We can find a peace in there that the world simply cannot give.

Jennifer enters that peaceful space by coloring mandalas and creating soothing art pieces; others have their own ways—keeping a moment of silence during a busy day, serving people who need support, walking mindfully, praying in a quiet church, journaling and many other ways that can help our spirits find stability within.

Our very breath can help us stay grounded in that space. Our awareness is usually dispersed onto many things (relationships, work, activities, and so on); through mindful slow inhalation and exhalation we can focus on the breath, letting distractions pass by like boats at sea without being controlled by them, increasing a sense of inner peace and reducing stress. As Rabbi Halozki notes, interior quietness also quiets the body.[11] Nevertheless, distracting thoughts still can pop up. Buddhist psychology and yogis capture this with the image of the "drunken monkeys."

Thoughts can move around, appear and disappear, like erratic monkeys swinging through trees. We need not be at the mercy of these thoughts; we can watch them pass as if we were spectators. By detaching ourselves from them we can then approach reality more freely, rather than being passive victims of whatever pops up within.

The space within can be accessed freely whether we believe in ourselves or not, whether we love ourselves or not, whether we are at peace with ourselves or not. Some may interpret this to be a space of emptiness, others may see it as a dimension of a cosmic energy with which we are all interconnected. Those who believe in God may see it as a space of unity with God since, as John of the Cross states, "God sustains every soul and dwells in it substantially, even though it may be that of the greatest sinner in the world. This union between God and creatures always exists."[12]

Being united with God means being united with love, since that is the very nature of God. No person or thing can separate us from love, which is by definition unconditional. The apostle Paul speaks poetically of this in his letter to the

Romans: "Neither death, nor life, nor angels, nor rulers, nor things present, nor things to come, nor powers,nor height, nor depth, nor anything else in all creation" can separate us from the love of God (8:38-39).

Nouwen spoke of God's love for us as the First Love—whatever we have experienced in our lives, this love has brought us into being and will last into eternity: "God has given you a beautiful self. There God dwells and loves you with the first love, which precedes all human love."[13]

God's first love for us is so fundamental (we come from it) and essential (it sustains us) that we can trust its voice calling us beloved. Describing the spiritual life to a Jewish friend, Nouwen writes: "Our many conversations led me to the inner conviction that the words, 'You are my Beloved' revealed the most intimate truth about all human beings, whether they belong any particular tradition or not. … All I hope is that you can hear these words as spoken to you with all the tenderness and force that love can hold."[14]

Letting God's eternal love touch our hearts can give us rest and free us to be who we are, consequently influencing the way we are in the world (transformation is primarily something that happens to us and that we therefore receive as we encounter love, rather than something we work on). The love of God trusts us. It sees us with tender eyes, exceeding the love a mother can have for her baby, and believes we can bring wonderful things into the world. In trusting us, it encourages us to trust in ourselves, as trust instills trust: when we know we are loved no matter what and seen as beautiful, in fact, not only can we rest and soak in such love, but we can also confidently trust and live out our deepest desires.

Some might consider believing in God too abstract, let alone basing their lives on God's love. Yet even if they don't believe in God, they can still believe in themselves, and might benefit from repeating to themselves Jennifer's words: "I believe in you." Indeed, loving ourselves is a profoundly human and spiritual step, whether we believe in God or not. Some may be open to the possibility that there is a God, even if they have questions or doubts. By living the virtue of hope (rather than seeking the attitude of certainty) they take the "risk" of trusting in the possibility of being radically loved by God, even if, at an emotional or intellectual level, their doubts remain.

We are always united to the abundant mystery of God's love, even if we may not be aware of it. Unsettling thoughts and changing moods can fill our minds with confusing ideas about who we are, distracting us from those loving and peaceful words that speak our truth: "You are the beloved." We can claim those sacred words within us by engaging in disciplines or practices that center us and bring us "beneath the surface," even if we might want to scream and cry (figuratively or literally) when superficial and diverting voices tell us otherwise.

Reconciling with Our History

A block (sometimes an aid!) to trusting in ourselves is our personal history. Personal past experiences affect how we live today. No wonder it is so important to reconcile with our history—its brighter side and its darker one, the loving parts and the unloving parts. Even if we can't change our past, we can savor its fruits and beautiful moments while also mourning what needs to be mourned, letting go of it without being enslaved by it.

I have already mentioned how we can trust only those we love, not those we are afraid of. Therefore, if we want to trust ourselves, we need to love ourselves. How to do so when some of our experiences may contradict our belovedness? When we become aware of personal and social histories of sickness, abuse, disasters, war and conflict, our identity as beloved loses its sentimentality and becomes a question in the form of a cry: "Are we really beloved?"

When she was younger, before coming to community, Karen lived in an institution with other people with disabilities. Still today, she mentions the horrible times she had to endure while institutionalized. She recalls, for example, getting out of the building only to go on a swing within its secluded grounds—that same swing from which someone once pushed her to the ground. She describes the institution as if it were an enclosed prison, with no possibility of escape. On the outskirts of a small city surrounded by vast cornfields, hidden from the public eye, in an alienating and overcrowded space (hundreds of people lived there), residents were subject to inconsiderate and cruel treatment by staff. Some even died of abuse.

In living community with her, we have befriended Karen and seek to reveal to her that she is valued and respected. When she has a need or wish, there is a group of friends ready to listen to her and support her. We want to provide Karen with a comfortable and safe environment, through the gentle way in which we look at her, our attentive ear and our non-threatening manner of speaking. We hope this approach helps her reconcile with her history, a process by which she can bring to light the various unresolved, confusing, and anguishing memories that still live within her and cause distress, while also realizing her preciousness.

Down through the years, since Karen has been out of the institution, one friendship that began in her early days of community, the one with assistant Alice, has helped her flourish. Alice, now married and living in a neighboring city, welcomes Karen to her home once a month. During their weekends together, Alice invites Karen to join her group of friends for downtown dinners and outings, which often involve shopping, hair styling, and going on walks with Alice's dog. Unlike the institution, where Karen's options were limited and her voice stifled, Alice offers Karen a variety of things to do together and encourages her to use her own voice in the choosing. By so doing Karen realizes that her wishes are important and that what she has to say needs to be heard.

The harshness of the past still haunts Karen. Memories of how she was treated and degraded still come back to Karen's mind, as if still fresh. During these flashbacks, we as community friends reiterate that even if some memories re-surface, she is now respected and that the past is behind her. Despite her having been oppressed, however, Karen remains a vocal catalyst for change. After leaving the institution, Karen attended a rally protesting its conditions and advocating that it close. As people became aware of the alarming reality within its walls through the local news, the institution finally shut down, eventually being used as a warehouse for a prison inmate labor program. After being hidden in a stifling context, Karen came out into the light advocating for its termination. Alice, who understood her pain and became her ally, joined her. By going to the rally, Karen was able to raise her voice and, in a way, "speak back" to that dark part of her history.

Even if we have never lived in an institution, looking back at certain painful memories may make us feel like victims of outside powers. The media presents us with stories of bullying in school, domestic violence, and other negative behaviors in which one person victimizes another. But we may also have experienced pain for reasons that don't make the news but stay with us—failed relationships, being disempowered at work by what our boss says to us, or opportunities that we looked forward to but that crumbled in the end. If not addressed, such wounds can remain open for a long time. Although we might think "the past is past," memories can shape how we view ourselves or others, affecting how we think and act in the present. Identifying our past hardships can help us claim the boundary between ourselves and the painful events that originated them, so that we can respond with more freedom, asserting our voice and even moving beyond them. For example, if a wrong and hurtful comment someone made a long time ago has stayed with us, we can admit that and put ourselves at a healthy distance from it by saying, "That comment they made was harsh. I still remember it after all this time. But this is me and that is them. What they said was not really about me but was about them and their insecurities." As we distance ourselves enough from the painful episode in our memory, we can untangle ourselves from its emotional power and feel empowered responding to it as needed instead of remaining passive victims of it.

Now that Karen has had time and distance from her former life and has learned to advocate for herself, she can keep growing in her sense of who she truly is, accepting that the terrible things she lived did not speak the truth about her. Step by step, she can free herself from the power of those tough memories, not pretending they never happened, but not letting them darken her present either.

Karen's personal history is also part of a larger social history that people with disabilities have experienced throughout the ages, facing rejection and violence. A short glance at disability history is quite telling. In ancient Rome, parents threw children with disabilities into the Tiber, while in the Middle Ages they were used as fools to entertain village fairgoers (or if they were female, sometimes burned as witches). In the nineteenth century they were locked away in asylums and institutions, sometimes even killed. Thanks to de-institutionalization policies and disability rights movements, there has been a positive shift toward community integration and inclusion, although people with disabilities remain one of the most forgotten and marginalized groups of society. Social attitudes are often more benevolent today, yet people with disabilities still face many attitudinal and structural barriers.

Their life histories are often painful. Babies with disabilities are frequently considered mistakes of nature, a pitiful misfortune for their parents. Knowing that a child in the womb is already sensitive to parental feelings and hormonal and chemical reactions, how much more will a baby's self-image and self-esteem be damaged if, already from within the womb, they are treated as a mistake. In modern society those with a disability might have the possibility of being schooled in inclusive classrooms and of a holding a job alongside people without disabilities. They might live in independent settings or in group homes within residential neighborhoods. At the same time, as Fiona Myers and other researchers have pointed out, they socially tend to remain "outside looking in,"[15] integrated in schools, workplaces, homes, and neighborhood but excluded from inclusive social relationships. Overall, the situation for many people with disabilities has improved in a variety of ways, but the heritage of suffering and injustice is an indelible part of their history.

Another core member, Jacob, entered community about the same time as Karen. Now he is a senior. Growing up in the South as an African American man with a disability, he faced discrimination. It still happens that individuals like Jacob, located at the intersection of ethnicity and disability, are considered inferior and are victimized by racist and ableist attitudes.

Jacob began living in L'Arche as an adult, and now speaks with the wisdom of one who has succeeded in integrating personal life experiences with practicality and spiritual meaning. More than once I have asked Jacob about his life story, and he always responds with interest. If this type of conversation takes place while he is at his community home, where he has many pictures and objects from his life, he usually takes out his family album to share images from his journey while offering descriptive photo commentaries. Picture after picture, page after page, Jacob shares about the countryside he grew up in and about his relationship with family members. At various times he has recalled the difficult relationship with his now deceased father, with whom he has yet to make peace. He has talked about his "white teacher" at school, acutely aware of the racial tensions that affected his younger years. His history, however, does not stop there—nor does it begin there. When he showed me a photo of himself in a formal setting, wearing a tuxedo next to his elegantly dressed mother, I could see in his eyes the affection that bonded him to her. Jacob also fondly reminisces, smiling warmly, about his closeness to his great-aunt, a source of comfort and teaching.

While browsing through the photo album, Jacob shares with pride the family traditions and cultural customs he learned as a child and that he remembers and treasures to this day, often keeping them alive within community. Thanks to Jacob, for example, I have discovered a dish that he enjoyed when he lived in the South. One morning, as he was quietly making breakfast before going to work, I saw him mixing white cornmeal in the pan, together with some honey. He explained that this was grits, a typical southern dish, and later taught me how to make it. At another moment, during a community event, he led a prayer ritual that he recollected as having Native American origins—a lit candle is passed around and upon receiving the candle each person is invited to move their hand in a circular motion above the flame.

Jacob has shared his history not only with me, but with many other people that he got to know in community. As he goes through his memories, he sometimes gets light and animated, as when describing moments shared with his great-aunt, while at other times he gets very serious, as when sharing about his dad. As he relates his history, Jacob exhibits a range of emotions depending on the people or moments recalled. He does not seem to edit out the painful parts, while also not forgetting the more cheerful moments. He is able to name, hold, and even share his history.

Our own histories are lived narratives that contain lighter and darker sides, which become memories. Our memories may contain pleasant images, interests, and customs experienced as youngsters, as Jacob has kept recipes from his great-aunt and spiritual practices from his southern upbringing; they can also carry fear and pain from unhappy events that can re-surface later on, like Karen's vivid re-imagining of being pushed from a swing in the institution. In some way, we are touched by every interaction we have engaged in, every event we have encountered, every flavor of life that we have tasted.

We can look at our past in its complexity, acknowledging our happier moments as well as those that have caused us sorrow. By doing so we recognize how it has influenced us, while also welcoming the newness of life that each day awaits us.

In seeking to understand how the past has affected us, thanks to psychology we can understand how critical for our development are our first five years of life. During that time, our brains change more and faster than at any other time. Our experiences—what we see, hear, touch, smell, and taste—stimulate the brain to create millions of connections, which become foundational for our growth. As adults we can reflect on and at times filter our experiences through critical thinking capacities, but as children we uncritically absorb what is around us, letting it shape us beyond our control. For example, suppose someone approaches us in a rude way. If that happens to us as adults we might think through that episode and interpret it, potentially imagining that maybe that person was just having a hard day or had bad manners. If that happens to us as children, instead, we will likely assume that we have caused that person's rudeness and that their behavior is our fault. How we are treated, held, and spoken to as infants reaches through us without filters, and informs (without necessarily determining) how we are going to behave in the future.

What we experienced in our infancy may not always be clear in our memory, but it is still inscribed in our bodies and present in our unconscious psyche. Reconciling with our histories does not necessarily mean dissecting everything that has ever happened to us, as if we have complete and clear cognitive access to our past; rather, it is an invitation to become conscious that quite a few of the inner dynamics, mechanisms and inclinations we exhibit today stem from memories (conscious or unconscious) of our younger years. If, for example, as babies in the womb or as young children we experienced our mother's relating to us as fundamentally anxious, it is not surprising if as adults we become prone to anxious responses in the face of life challenges. If, on the other hand, our attachment to her was secure and safe, we are likely to feel encouraged to explore life and the world with a spirit of trust rather than fear.

We may not realize how the past is still present within us and how ready it is to emerge in unexpected ways. In listening to assistants that begin their community journey, I have noticed that they have some awareness of the challenges people with disabilities have had to face throughout history, and they want to be positive agents of change in their lives. It is interesting, however, to witness how interacting with core members often brings these well-intentioned assistants face-to-face with their own pasts and their own needs! Carolina, for example, was an assistant who came from Latin America to the community house where core member Jennifer lived. At first Carolina, still adjusting to the new culture and language, had a hard time understanding Jennifer's speech and eruptive behaviors, and grew frustrated in not knowing how to interact with her and consequently how to support her well. One evening, however, something happened that touched Carolina to the core. She was finishing something in the kitchen and Jennifer, who was there as well, attentively told her, "Did you eat something today? I didn't see. Go eat something." As Jennifer told her these caring words, Carolina was reminded of how she was treated back home by her mother, who was far away and whose concern Jennifer unexpectedly echoed. This moved Carolina deeply. Through a simple demonstration of caring love, Jennifer awakened Carolina's past within her present, bringing her back to her mother's presence and to the warm sense of home that Carolina had left. Who would have thought that the core member who Carolina had such a challenging time with would also be the one to awaken in her the warm and sweet memory of her mother's love?

In relationship with others, we are likely to encounter triggers that bring us in touch with the memories from our past, wanted or unwanted. Although assistants like Carolina often find their arrival in community to be a joyous and novel time of orientation, I have observed how the initial days are such a novel experience for them that many resort to coping mechanisms learned in the past, helpful or unhelpful. Suddenly, they find themselves in a new home, living with strangers with different personalities and backgrounds, not understanding their place in all of this. Many are confident in navigating this newness as it unfolds, showing great flexibility and openness to the new, while others feel more displaced in trying to establish themselves. As their own insecurities emerge, they may give in to compulsions learned in their pasts. They may, for example, get frustrated at themselves if they don't understand the ways of their housemates or if they don't learn things quickly, a pressure they probably put on themselves because in their prior life experiences they learned that they had to be efficient and in control. These assistants are invited to be kind with themselves, and to be forgiving towards whatever it is that upsets them from within. When we forgive ourselves (and others), we can accept not always meeting our expectations while also moving forward.

One of the assistants I welcomed in community, Stefan, once honestly expressed how he wasn't sure what kind of person he needed to be around the core members and assistants with whom he had begun to live. He felt that they already knew each other well enough as they had been living together for some time and that, as much as he wanted them to like and welcome him, he didn't feel part of their group. This insecurity created an inner anxiety. He did not believe in himself and did not trust that he was enough as he was. Stefan was prone to depression and was hard on himself (yet very sympathetic with others). He wanted to fit in with the group but did not know how. As I listened, I encouraged Stefan to simply be who he was, as his gift to community was to be himself—the person we chose to welcome—and not someone else! I believed in Stefan. A kindhearted and reflective person, from the moment I met him I thought he would be a great presence in community and time and time again I sought to affirm that.

Stefan's insecurity, however, did not come from nowhere; it was symptomatic of something deeper. At a younger age, in fact, it seems that Stefan had exhibited a similar behavior—in order to fit in with his peers he felt the pressure of needing to prove he was "someone," so as to be appreciated by them. That memory easily gets triggered upon joining new groups, even within an accepting community. As a child did Stefan learn that love needed to be earned and that he had to change himself to be worthy of it? His behaviors seemed to suggest that pattern. Did he not feel appreciated as he was? If we don't feel appreciated for who we are, we can try changing ourselves to deserve love, which of course defeats its very notion.

As Stefan's time in community continued, a transformation started to happen. As he lived with core members who were very much themselves around him, without filters, Stefan began to see that they could be themselves, and so could he. At first, he wanted to be a friendly and engaging presence around the house, but he eventually became content to be truly himself without pretenses, particularly jolly at times and feeling low at other times. He initially worried that his cooking was not good enough, but he eventually could smile about his culinary skills and prepare dinners that were fine enough (by the time he left, they were excellent). He came having professional goals for the future weighting on his mind; eventually he could trust that things would unfold anyway without him needing to obsess over them.

During his months alongside core members and other assistants, Stefan took time for self-reflection and, as he pondered on journey, was able to distance himself from the compulsion to be liked that he inherited from his past and was able to speak back to it, recognizing that it was not serving him well and growing in confidence, aware of his insecurities while slowly letting them go. He became comfortable as Stefan, speaking and acting as himself, and not as an ideal image of that someone he imagined other people wanted to be around.

From time to time Stefan's past insecurities resurfaced again but no longer held him hostage. He was freer. His inclination to depression did not magically disappear, but in opening himself to loving and joyful relationships with others, new life lightened up his spirit. By the time he transitioned from home life to university studies, not only had the community believed in him, which had been the case since the day he moved in, but he believed in himself, too.

Reconciling with our past allows our beings to emerge through the positive and the harder moments of our lives, through loving memories and harsher ones, and through those inherited behaviors and ways of thinking that we want to keep and those that we want to let go. It is a journey that can be challenging, but also one that can lead to freedom.

Embracing Our Abilities and Inabilities

Believing in ourselves is different than pride and self-aggrandizement, which inflate our sense of self and therefore distance us from how we truly are. Rather, it is connected to humility, a word that comes from the Latin "humus," meaning earth or soil: to trust ourselves we need to be realistic about the possibilities and limits inscribed in our beings. We can do so by embracing our abilities and all that we can do with our lives, but as finite human beings also our inabilities and all that we are not able to do. Embracing our abilities can enhance our potential and refine our skills. Embracing our inabilities, on the other hand, can transform us into complete and connected human beings; when we cannot do something, we can accept our human limitedness and can ask others to support us, growing in relationship with them.

Our cultural climate encourages us to become "the best," emphasizing success no matter what. But such a bloated vision of growth makes "super-heroes" out of humans and is therefore unhealthy. As individuals on this earth we do have innate potential, wonderful capacities, and untapped abilities. Yet we simply cannot do it all; we have our own inabilities.

Jacob, besides his ability to hold and share his story that we have previously encountered, also has another—music-making. When friends and guests come to visit at his community home, he often invites them to stand by him in the living room as he plays impromptu tunes on his keyboard. Jacob, who also plays as his local church, has quite a talent in creating songs on the spot, and he speaks with pride about a music CD he made years ago to preserve and share some of his musical creations. This ability, which is stimulating and enjoyable to him, also lets him bring joy and lightness to others.

At this point in his life, Jacob is also coming to terms with some of his inabilities, such as not being able to remember things as well as he may want. This is a part of his aging that he is learning to accept. It is also calling forth community—when Jacob forgets, his friends can help him remember. I recall, for example, when we visited a disability services office to arrange for his transportation. When the employee asked him for his house address, Jacob concentrated as he tried to guess the right house number. His expression, thoughtful and somewhat confused, seemed to say, "I don't remember my house address. I can't do it." I, however, could support him, providing the address to the staff person and helping Jacob re-learn that information.

As he gets older, Jacob also has trouble moving around the city safely during wintery nights. Years ago, no matter the weather, he could walk to buses or trains on his commute to and from work. He eventually realized, as his vision and mobility deteriorated, that he would benefit from a door-to-door transportation service, which he now uses.

As we age, our family, educational, and social contexts develop, and so do our abilities and skills. Some people, for example, might have abilities in intellectual analysis, in practical skills or, like Jacob's improv music creation, in artistic endeavors. Some people might be particularly gifted in their relational abilities, for example being able to lead constructive group conversations or having heightened empathy to others' feelings. Whether acquired or inherited, our abilities relate to what we can do well.

Our inabilities, on the other hand, concern what we can't do, or can't do well. In our current socio-cultural milieu, inabilities are framed as opportunities for growth, transient realities to work on, or as steppingstones by which they can be turned into abilities. For example, children who have an inability to think numerically might be encouraged to pay extra attention in math class so that the inability might turn into an ability. Family members might respond to older persons who forget having done an activity they just performed with, "Don't you remember?", hoping that statement could be a wake-up call to restore their ability to recall.

In our families, schools, and workplaces we have been encouraged—sometimes even pressured—to develop our abilities. The famous slogan, "Yes, you can!" is a clear encouragement to develop one's abilities and to do something well. Our society values ability and consequently rewards it. When we do things well we receive affirmation and positive feedback. When we get good grades at school, excel at sports, or bring positive results in the workplace, we receive promotions of different kinds. Unable to understand a language? Unable to understand your psyche? Unable to figure out financial matters? A course, a therapeutic session, or a consultation can turn those inabilities into abilities.

There is nothing wrong with wanting to do things well and to develop and maintain our abilities that can make a unique difference in the world. This, however, does not need to devalue inability as being less important or relevant. Welcoming our inabilities—what we can't do—can be as enriching as developing our abilities.

By integrating our inabilities, we become more complete human beings because we learn to accept a fuller version of ourselves, not only the productive and successful part. In addition, we also call forth community when we invite others to lend their own abilities to support us in what we can't do. When we do something well it is easy to rely on ourselves and just "get it done," but when we cannot do something we can ask other human beings and God: "I need you. Can you help me?" We can create community. No wonder Nouwen used to speak of community as a fellowship of the weak:[16] if we could do everything by ourselves we wouldn't need others.

We all have inabilities, simply by virtue of being human. None of us can change our history or our biological make-up. We may have physical or psychological inabilities, some practical (as in the inability to perform certain tasks in a certain way) and some emotional (as in the inability to be vulnerable or to let things go). We may have had some inabilities since birth, while others may have entered our lives at a different time. Some inabilities might be minor or secondary, while others more profound and critical.

Personally, I find various abilities within myself, including the ability to connect with others and the ability to be patient with people. Alongside my abilities, however, I have inabilities, one of which I had to face in an unexpected way. Some time ago, late on a springtime night, I was feeling quite sick, restless and unable to sleep. My throat was sore, my fever was high, and my mind busy. At a certain point, I became aware of a strange movement taking place within my body. As I felt this strange cardiac motion I had never experienced before I was not sure what to do. I did not understand what was happening, and I could not control it. As I felt increasingly dizzy, I got up from bed and knocked on my housemate's door for help, only to faint on the floor after a few seconds. After I regained consciousness, my housemate took me to the emergency room. After the medical staff reviewed my electrocardiogram, I realized that something serious was happening as the doctor and various nurses rushed into the room. As one of the nurses was about to give me aspirin, she told me I was having a heart attack. Fully conscious and aware, I was catapulted into shock and intense fear. As I lay on the stretcher, anguished and apprehensive, I kept looking to the nurses for a word of comfort or encouragement. I wanted to hear that my heart was going to get better, a certitude they could not give me. I stayed in the hospital for a couple of days while the doctors continued to monitor and treat me. It turned out that my arteries did not have any blockage and that what I had experienced was technically not a heart attack, although some symptoms were similar.

While under observation at the hospital, I was touched that, upon receiving news of my hospitalization, an intimate community of friends visited me to show their care. They stayed by my hospital bed and brought me things that I needed during my stay. There was a bond among us. Upon hearing what had happened one friend brought me socks and a phone charger. Another asked me what I wished to eat, cooked it, and served it to me the next day. She covered the hospital tray with a small tablecloth, beautifying the sterile hospital space.

My parents flew in from out of state to be with me for days as I re-adjusted and processed what had happened.

My heart suffered some immediate consequences from the event, but during the subsequent months of rest and recovery, it was able to heal, leaving that episode a memory of the past. I have not forgotten, however, the intense sense of inability I experienced: in the emergency room, I knew something out of the ordinary was happening, but in the face of it I felt powerless. I could not control my body. I could not really control my life, either; in the face of nature's mysterious cycle what I could "control" was small. Life and death were not in my hands. Rationally, I already knew that, up to a certain extent, I could shape my life without having full control over it, as living runs its course without asking for our permission. In the hospital, however, this stopped being just an obvious reasonable insight, but became a confounding physical experience.

Accepting our inabilities does not come automatically or easily. This interior stance might only be developed through suffering or at least through a humbling experience by which we recognize the reality of our human limits and that we cannot do it all on our own. For some, coming to terms with this truth can lead to crisis or profound disappointment. I think of Meredith, mother of one of our community's core members, who developed Alzheimer's disease. Becoming aware that she could no longer remember things as she used to, that she possibly would forget everything as time progressed, shocked her.

Psychotherapist David Richo describes crisis using the image of a desert: "The landscape of the human psyche, like that of the earth, includes desert places. They are parched not by the sun, wind, and fire but by weakness, helplessness, and hopelessness. When we find ourselves in such a crisis, we can pause mindfully with no attempt to fill anything in—as a desert is an acceptable pause in the ecology."[17] Inabilities can create a desert space in our psyche where we come face to face with everything that we can't be and everything we can't do. In such a space we may feel weak and empty, longing to fill it with ability, power, health, or success, all those things that can make us feel "in charge." Such deserts, nonetheless, invite us to come to terms with our basic human finitude. It also spurs us to find our personal oases, reaching out for inner resources and relationships that support us when we cannot do it on our own.

By developing our abilities, we grow in our skills and talents. By welcoming our inabilities, we accept our limitedness and need for others. Believing in ourselves is an opportunity to trust in both, letting them show us how stimulating and empowering it is to develop our abilities but also how profoundly human and bonding not being able to do something can be.

Accepting Our Bodies

Your cognitive capacities allow you to understand these pages and reflect critically on the stories and information they contain, but it is your eyes that see these black words printed on white pages; it is your fingers that hold and flip through them (or if you have an audio version, your ears are listening to their content). Reading might seem like an intellectual endeavor, but it is an act based on the body. The brain itself is made up of physical gray matter; even what we refer to as "mind"—our intellectual faculty—is rooted in physicality. In a similar way, believing in ourselves is not simply an abstract act, a few clever brain tricks. Belief in self is deeply embodied. It invites us to be present and alive in our bodies, whereby we can know ourselves better and come to terms with the grandeur and vulnerability of our lives.

People with developed intellectual abilities can often hide behind ideas, living in their heads and alienating themselves from the truth expressed by their bodies. During my time in L'Arche, however, I had the privilege of knowing people with intellectual disabilities who, in my experience, commonly hide much less behind their thoughts than the "general population" while remaining close to their embodied reality. One of these is Lucia, a woman with Down syndrome.

Lucia is not able to speak and may often be found sitting on the house couch, rocking her torso back and forth, holding some of her fingers in her mouth while moving and staring at the others. When I lived with her in community, I would often sit next to Lucia, just to be present to her. She would do what she often did with her friends—either take my hand gently to hold it or aggressively grab my scarf, if I was wearing one. Sometimes Lucia would even take people by the hand and walk with them.

Lucia's embodied communication is not always easy to understand. Is there something she'd like to convey as she takes people by the hand and walks with them? What is she thinking when she affectionately holds their hands as she rocks back and forth? How does Lucia feel when she forcefully pulls people's scarves (or watches!) and doesn't let go? There is an element of mystery in her non-verbal expression. Sometimes it seems to rise from a surge of affection; other times it seems to change abruptly into a cry of anguish. Although I have known her for some time, I am still learning the language of Lucia.

Today we cannot escape virtual reality, with its great and challenging aspects. From emails to social media, a substantial part of the world's population—at least those who can connect to the internet— has been able to communicate in a way that had been unthinkable. With nearby neighbors, with those on the other side of the world, people can share ideas, create interest groups, form elective communities, and even come together for socio-political change. Besides being undeniably efficient and convenient, however, online communication lacks physicality. Although emails or text messages are effective and immediate, they don't convey the physical quality of the writer's voice or the singularity of their handwriting. Emoticons and emojis can translate a feeling into an icon, but they don't reveal the sender's facial expression and body language—nor those of the receiver upon opening the message. Regardless, virtual communication has become a staple of the modern era.

Lucia does not live in a virtual world. The way she passes time, her interactions and communication style happen close to her body, within a specific geographic location, with the external world that surrounds her. Lucia communicates primarily through her hands, her deep dark brown eyes, and her non-verbal sounds. Lucia makes new friends by taking them by the hand, without any media filters. Her hands, at times gentle and at times harsh, reveal forces of disarming candor and powerful strength, with a physical clarity that electronic devices cannot convey.

Throughout history, numerous thinkers have identified reason as the trait that differentiates human beings from animals. Aristotle considered human beings rational animals, while for Cicero intelligence and reason were humankind's supreme qualities, shared with the gods; The Cartesian approach that emphasizes existence in connection with thinking has profoundly influenced Western philosophy. People like Lucia, but also those whose memory is fading (as in people experiencing dementia) or people with brain injury, bring into question this limited way of defining people in terms of their mental capacity.

Affirming the primacy of the intellect over other human faculties creates an unhealthy division between mind and body. It is not surprising that in modern culture people who have grown tired of living in their heads are increasingly becoming aware of the "mind/body connection," which may account for the increased popularity of mindfulness and yoga exercises. Feeling distant from our bodies makes us crave the need to feel unity between mind, body, and spirit. Each of us already embodies this unity, whether we realize it or not. All the layers of our being are already integrated; we don't need to create that unity, rather just live it. Our thoughts are influenced by our biological reactions, our bodily sensations by our thoughts, and our spiritual side by our thoughts and feelings. Indeed, the ways in which our thoughts are influenced by our biology and how our emotional and spiritual lives influence our thinking and our physical states cannot be quantified, although all are at play within us.

The life of Lucia "speaks" quite a bit through her physical communication, as does the life of Jesus. The gospel does not present a God who remains a sterile spirit in the world of ideas, but a God who becomes incarnate: born as a little baby in a specific town (Bethlehem) within a poor family (we can imagine him moving his tiny feet and hands as Mary and Joseph held him), approaching people and healing them with his physical touch, asking a woman for water when he was thirsty, inviting people to join him for breakfast on the seashore, touching marginalized people like the leper and the woman with a hemorrhage, washing his friends' tired feet, sharing bread, bleeding to death on a cross, rising not only in spirit but also in body—all out of love. A love that has eyes, hands, feet, and a heartbeat.

The church draws its sacramental vision from the incarnation: we don't become "spiritual" by leaving the body; rather the spiritual is revealed through our bodies, the things of nature, the world. Nikos Kazantzakis, Greek author from Crete, reflected, "Within me even the most metaphysical problem takes on a warm physical body which smells of sea, soil, and human sweat. The Word, in order to touch me, must become warm flesh. Only then do I understand—when I can smell, see, and touch."[18] The apostle Paul, in his letter to Christians in Corinth, reminds them that the body is a temple of the Holy Spirit (1 Cor 6:19). I find this quite touching; it feels like good news. From experience, in fact, I know I want to be close to my loved ones and, as much as I appreciate being able to communicate with distant friends via phone or video calling, I feel how much better it is to have them close to me, look into their eyes, see their body language, give them an embrace. In a similar vein, God is not close to us merely as a spirit whose words we can read and whose presence we can imagine but as an incarnate presence who is deeply in tune with our fundamental human need for relationship and intimacy, as God's mysterious presence in the eucharistic bread and wine points to.

In the Gospel of Matthew, Jesus surprises his followers when he tells them, "For I was hungry and you gave me food, I was thirsty and you gave me something to drink, I was a stranger and you welcomed me, I was naked and you gave me clothing, I was sick and you took care of me, I was in prison and you visited me" (25: 35-36). They did not remember ever doing this to him and were confused. He replied by sharing with them how he is present in the body of the poor: "Just as you did it to one of the least of these who are members of my family, you did it to me" (40).

The spiritual life, therefore, takes the body seriously—God's body and the body of our humanity. This is not a foreign concept in other religious traditions either. In Judaism, for example, a life of *shalom*, the Hebrew word for peace, does not only mean absence of war, but speaks of completeness, of a general feeling of physical and spiritual well-being. The *zazen* (literally, "seated meditation") practice of Zen Buddhism encourages a specific sitting posture and breathing focus as part of its meditative discipline.

Throughout history, however, the body has often been treated skeptically, if not badly, because of philosophical worldviews that downplayed it. For example, the Platonic understanding that the body is a prison of the soul. Questionable religious understandings also devalue the body. For example, Paul reflects on the difference between spirit and flesh, a differentiation easily misunderstood as a dichotomy in which the spirit is considered good and the body bad. As David Steindl-Rast explains, however, in the ancient Near East, when animals were slaughtered, their parts had to be processed quickly lest the flesh rot in the heat. In this context, "flesh" signifies what is spoiled, whereas "spirit" refers to the breath of life. The contrast between spirit and flesh, therefore, is meant to express the power of vitality over mortality, a vitality that of course includes the aliveness of our bodies; it does not suggest that the spirit is the opposite of the body, let alone that the body is bad![19]

Besides being disregarded, the body can also be devalued by being conceived as meaningless and de-personalized. When it is exploited as an instrument or tool, divorced from the interior life of the individual, its holistic dimension is disdained. A person is a body, but not just a body. Each human being is a unique union of emotional, spiritual, and intellectual energies. Hence, when we interact with someone's body we are not just seeing or touching their skin; we are seeing or touching their person.

In living community with others, our bodily communication has the capacity to express the care with which we treat them as people and what we want to reveal to them. Pope Francis writes how, "The Son of God, by becoming flesh, summoned us to the revolution of tenderness."[20] Tenderness implies treating people respectfully, kindly, maturely, gently and in a humble way that profoundly affirms their dignity. It creates a relational space where the other is honored. It is the opposite of violence of any kind. Pope Francis presents Mary as an icon of tenderness, mentioning how in her example one can see "that humility and tenderness are not virtues of the weak but of the strong who need not treat others poorly in order to feel important themselves."[21]

Tenderness is caring and shows others that we value them; not controlling nor possessing, it is grounded in respect. It is expressed in the way we look at people, in how we listen to them, in the tone of our voice, in the way we touch them, in our demeanor as we are with them, and even in how we relate to the world at large. When we treat ourselves tenderly, we live out those same qualities towards our very being. The stance of tenderness—that loving respect made manifest in gentleness—can free us to be who we are. It provides a safe and sensitive space for growth. Dietrich von Hildebrand explains that all categories of love include tender affectivity, which displays itself in "being moved."[22] Such tenderness presents itself in various forms—in one's relationship towards self, in that between family members, among friends, among partners and spouses, and between the person and God.

At L'Arche, tenderness is revealed through the attention given to the needs of the core members. I think, for example, of assistant Sheena and core member Caroline. Caroline tends to personalize objects and talk to them. From wishing goodnight to the community bicycle to speaking to the toaster, Caroline not only uses, but also interacts with the material things around her. Although people that don't know Caroline may consider her behavior disturbed, Sheena, who has lived with her for years, understands Caroline and knows the things she cares about. Whenever Caroline speaks to household items, Sheena is present to her with a tender stance: she delicately converses with Caroline, therefore encouraging human connection over talking to objects, while understanding where Caroline is at and how she sees the world. She does not force her viewpoint on Caroline nor make her feel ashamed. Her presence is tender, merging kindness of stance and strength of belief in Caroline's preciousness. I also think of Ted, and how, when we lived as housemates, I took turns with other assistants in helping him with his morning and night routines, including washing his hair and shaving his beard. When I shampooed his hair, I sought to do so with delicate, patient hands so he could feel I was treating him as a precious human being. When I shaved his beard I took care not to nick him with the razor when he would move his mouth. Other assistants took care in supporting Ted and they, too, looked at him and touched him with a delicacy that upheld his dignity. This obviously is not the tenderness between a parent and a child nor the romantic one between lovers, but a tender stance between friends or between a caregiver and the person being supported.

In our own lives, we may not notice our own lack of attention to bodily needs and wisdom. Eating too quickly, walking too fast, or wanting to appear busy at all costs may signify inattention to rhythms of the body. Sometimes I see people who look tired but are still "on the go," maintaining their activity although they seem ready to doze off at any moment. Their demeanor reveals a disconnect between mental activity and physical state, a disjunction between mind and body. Putting our bodies under so much stress can start to seem ordinary until our bodies fall sick and demand our attention.

Appointments, worries at work, media information overload, and not taking time to gather ourselves can add up and damage our bodies. Surrounded by stimuli, we can begin to be over-sensitive to them and react to them as threats—to be faced or to be fled from. This automatic "red-alert mode" is created in the amygdala, the brain structure connected with emotional response, particularly fear. When stress hormones are released, they lead to faster heart beats, higher blood pressure, and more rapid breathing, which make rest or sleep difficult. This stress-response reflex can be life-saving when we are at risk and quickly need to choose the best course of action. Becoming too used to such a high level of alertness and stress, however, even when our lives are not in peril (like finding many emails in our mailbox or arriving late at a meeting), can inhibit our immune system, get us sick, and make us feel depleted. It can alienate us from the needs of our bodies, which plead for tender care but receive only more pressure.

The ways to take care of our bodies are many. We know, for example, that slow deep breathing helps lower our heart rate, adequate sleep helps with healing and longevity, maintaining a healthy diet keeps us physically and mentally fit, and physical activity (even walking) stimulates the production of mood-enhancing endorphins that can both lift one's mood and be calming.

Our bodies also hide a wisdom, which if listened to can be quite telling. In decision-making, we often turn to our reason—"What do I think about it?" But asking ourselves "How do I feel about it?" lets us tap into the intuition and wisdom of our physicality. Although we often rationalize about the issues we face (weighting pros and cons, thinking through different possibilities, abstracting a lesson from them), it is important that we not overlook how they make us feel in our bodies.

When I took a course that explored the underpinnings and practice of emotion-focused therapy, I learned how a person can better understand the issues they might be dealing with by focusing on the emotions that they experience. During a role-play, I played the role of a client while the professor, acting as the therapist, provided me with emotion-focused therapy. During the session, he asked me about my emotions, encouraging me to put into words how they felt, where I sensed them in my body, and what reactions I experienced during the process. I consider myself quite in tune with my real feelings. Nevertheless, even though this was only a simulation (I could make something up without experiencing what I was describing), I was surprised at how challenging it was to describe emotions in their physicality. This role-play helped me reflect on how we are not used to describe our feelings with the same nuance that we use to describe our thoughts. We have never been taught a vast grammar of emotional self-expression. I had to learn it (and am still learning it) on my own, finding words for my experience and noticing how others do it. We need to build up our emotional literacy!

Our bodies bear an irrepressible honesty, communicating better than language. Whether we consciously choose to or not, body language can show our true intentions and sentiments, more honestly than words do. We can use words to reveal or to conceal ourselves, but our feelings, whether clear or confusing, tend to be forthright. Have you ever tried to convey something you didn't fully mean and your bodily expressions couldn't get behind that facade? Have you ever watched someone describe how excited they are in life, yet their gaze wanders around the room, their hands moving nervously and their expression remaining pensive? The weight that body language carries is so significant that entire fields of study focus on it.

Our bodies, bearing our personal histories and memories, are a source of knowledge about ourselves. Some body memories seem almost ingrained in our physical way of being—for example, we re-enact the way we speak or the way we move as if it were natural, but both are something we have learned through time. Some memories stored in the body, instead, can be painful, like the pang that is re-lived when a traumatic event is recalled, such as victims of abuse who may feel overwhelmed when visiting the place in which their abuse took place, or victims of war feeling panic at the sound of loud noises. Other memories have pleasant undertones, as when beautiful experiences from childhood get re-awakened in the present. In his masterpiece *In Search of Lost Time*, Marcel Proust embarks on a stream-of-consciousness recollection based on his lifetime of sense perceptions. One well-known moment involves him dunking a small madeleine sponge-cake in tea and being catapulted to his younger years through the memory of its taste and texture:

> I raised to my lips a spoonful of the tea in which I had soaked a morsel of the cake. No sooner had the warm liquid mixed with the crumbs touched my palate than a shudder ran through me and I stopped, intent upon the extraordinary thing that

> was happening to me. An exquisite pleasure had invaded my senses, something isolated, detached, with no suggestion of its origin. ... Whence could it have come to me, this all-powerful joy? ... Undoubtedly what is thus palpitating in the depths of my being must be the image, the visual memory which, being linked to that taste, is trying to follow it into my conscious mind ... And suddenly the memory revealed itself. The taste was that of the little piece of madeleine which on Sunday mornings at Combray (because on those mornings I did not go out before mass), when I went to say good morning to her in her bedroom, my aunt Léonie used to give me, dipping it first in her own cup of tea or tisane.[23]

Proust's recollection transcends cognition; a physical experience opened up memories and experiences, so much so that "in that moment all the flowers in our garden and in M. Swann's park, and the water-lilies on the Vivonne and the good folk of the village and their little dwellings and the parish church and the whole of Combray and its surroundings, taking shape and solidity, sprang into being, town and gardens alike, from my cup of tea."[24]

Our bodies all differ: some taller, some shorter, some thinner, some chubbier, some move by walking, some move via a wheelchair, some with four limbs, some with fewer. Our bodies can feel fresh, energized and healthy, but they can also feel old, tired and sick. Some bodies carry visible scars from difficult experiences, some carry these scars inside. Some bodies have been touched gently, treated with care, and held safely; others have been violently grabbed or abandoned. Every-body is both fragile and strong.

Core member Francis endured many hospitalizations, his body needing a lot of medical attention and care. One milestone in his life was receiving a donated kidney. Before that transplant surgery Francis needed dialysis. He lived close to the brokenness of the human body—its poverty and its vulnerability—yet also to its incredible power. Each year he celebrated his kidney anniversary, both in person with friends and via social media posts, affirming the power of life and resilience. He was aware of his body's needs. Because he was prone to epilepsy, at night he needed a seizure alert monitor. When he watched a movie, he avoided strong visual stimuli. Although Francis had to endure such physical issues, he was a living witness to the body's capacity to heal itself and move forward with trust. At birth, it was predicted that he would live only a few weeks; he lived almost into his forties.

In people like Francis—and in our own bodies—we encounter life's magnificence and its vulnerability. Our bodies function with such miraculous meticulousness that it is easy to take for granted our waking up each day, our continuous breathing, our constant heartbeat, our immune system that keeps us alive and fights for us. At the same time, we are also susceptible to illness, diminishing strength, and, ultimately, death. Although it is hard to comprehend this mystery through reason, our bodies themselves contain the paradoxical interplay of life and death. By the age of thirteen the theologian and sociologist Nancy L. Eiesland had lived through eleven operations for a congenital bone defect in her hips. She described Jesus as a disabled God who, even in his risen glorified body, appeared to his disciples with wounded hands and feet, calling "his frightened companions to recognize in the marks of impairment their own connection with God, their own salvation."[25] The image of Jesus' wounded hands and feet reveals the splendor of humanity—not sterile and picture-perfect, but hidden in our beautiful and vulnerable bodies.

Our bodies reveal our grandeur and our finitude. Physical and instinctual memories and sensations express where we have been, where we are, and what we need. Within community I came to know people with intellectual disabilities who did not hide behind thoughts and intellectual constructs. They were close to the truth that their bodies expressed. Living fully through the body, however, is not just for a selected few; it is an invitation for all. To trust in ourselves we have to discover, heed, and listen attentively to our bodies' voice and wisdom.

Following Our Inner Voice

Believing in ourselves is an invitation to listen to and follow our own unique inner voice, even if this sometimes brings us into conflict with what others expect from us. We are the protagonists of our lives and if we put responsibility for our decisions and actions onto others, we give them power over our lives. Making space for our inner voice and having the courage to follow it implies a risk—we don't know how things will turn out. Thankfully, we don't need to have everything figured out before moving forward; we can trust that by following our inner voice things will turn out well.

My story of moving into L'Arche is one of following my inner voice, even if it did involve some risk. When I was finishing my undergraduate degree, I began reading about L'Arche through publications and websites. Struck by its novel way of living simple community with people who have intellectual disabilities and sensing within myself an invitation to join L'Arche as a school of life, I began to look more into it. I traveled to two North American communities to see them in real life so I could understand what I might be living there.

I did not doubt my desire to join L'Arche. I knew that it was a fit and I wanted to be part of it. However, I wasn't sure which of the two communities to join. As I walked through the homes, joining dinners and meeting community members, I remained in touch with what I was sensing within. Although the first community I visited was located in a more vibrant and exciting city, I would have been asked to hold responsibility as a house team member sooner (too soon, I thought) than in the second. The second community, located in a smaller suburban area, felt relaxed and down to earth. I wouldn't have chosen one or the other solely based on location, but since I liked both I needed to weigh the different aspects in making my decision. Both communities were ready to welcome me. Balancing the two options, I sensed a bit more joy in considering the second, which is the one that I selected. Once I made a choice, I was happy and did not look back.

Ever since, I have been part of L'Arche communities in various countries. I still remember traveling to small-town France to see where this international inclusive community movement started: I sensed a need to follow this desire to go there even with a limited knowledge of French (once there, at first it was quite hard to understand others and I imagine how hard it was for them to understand my sentences in broken basic French!). Before arriving, I felt some resistance from outside to the idea of joining a community far away, yet I was convinced within. Some of my family and friends were supportive and encouraging, but I did receive some push-back; this was also the case with the first community I joined in North America. Wherever in the world, why would I go live with people with disabilities when, having graduated with good grades, I could find a "real job" and make more money? In a cultural milieu that values upward mobility—getting to the top of the social ladder while keeping others at the bottom—going to live with marginalized people, especially after investing time and resources in an education, seemed strange. Nevertheless, I knew that I had to go there; my inner voice had convinced me to follow that direction. This inner voice helped me stay grounded even through those moments of weariness and wanting to leave for a more familiar place that made the first months in community particularly challenging. Eventually, also thanks to small ordinary moments like helping a core member with his weekly pasta cooking and getting to know many international volunteers, the experience revealed itself to be very formative, through the enjoyable moments and the more tiring ones. I am glad I followed what I wanted to do, even if it initially wasn't understood by everyone.

In my personal example, following my inner voice meant moving to a community home with housemates I had never met before, with differing abilities and disabilities, but it also meant leaving it when the time came. This experience of transition I shared with most assistants, who also came to live in for a determinate amount of time, but also with some core members, like Katie, a young lady in her early twenties who moved into L'Arche after residing with her parents. When Katie first arrived to community as a visitor, she seemed enthusiastic, excited, and ready to be part of it. During the initial welcome process, we met with her and with her parents. We wanted her to know more about our living practices and structures, but we also wanted to hear how she felt about joining community, what she enjoyed doing, and how we could ease her transition into this new context.

Upon entering, Katie seemed to get along with her five new housemates and expressed liking for her new living arrangement. While partaking in community life, she kept developing the relationships she already had with friends and colleagues around the city. We wanted to support the life-giving connections she had outside of the home—a community should not be closed and inward looking, but always flowing outside of itself. As the months progressed, however, she seemed to disengage from community members and find more life in activities with her other friends. Unsurprisingly, Katie began to express interest in other living options and perhaps in moving out of L'Arche.

Katie's parents were sad that she wanted to leave our community and live somewhere else. They liked the person-centered and warm spirit in her home, and they did not think that other group homes in the area could provide those important elements. They tried to talk her out of it, sought to convey the risks of such a decision, but Katie, a young adult ready to explore new possibilities, wanted to decide for herself. She made appointments to visit other residential contexts, while her mother lost sleep over her wandering.

I and other community members wanted Katie to know that she was welcome to stay in L'Arche while she explored other living options, and that she was free to decide if she needed a change. Although some felt more protective, hoping she would decide to stay, it was evident that she wanted something else. Those of us who are older than Katie might remember what it felt like to discover in our early twenties that we could choose among different life possibilities, even if this meant testing them through trial and error. Eventually Katie did find another agency serving people with disabilities that offered to welcome her into one of their group homes, and she opted to move there.

As we make decisions, an inner sense can help us recognize why one thing may or may not be better for us than another. That is our inner voice. This nudge from within does not feel forced but is a personal conviction that one choice instead of another makes the most sense. How do I tell my friends that what they did upset me? Should I make a career change? Can I commit to a certain activity at this point? Whatever the question, when we feel that a particular answer fits what we are looking for, we know it and it is hard to deny. Our inner voice can also present itself when we don't have a particular question in mind or a decision to make. People can sense a conviction to enter a relationship, to commit to a social justice issue, or to make a life change, without planning and without expectation. Although our inner voice is not always clear and self-evident, it is always there, to be heeded and to be followed, for us to live our true selves without regret.

Our inner voice provides inner knowledge and guidance. Some know it as "conscience," from the Latin *conscientia*, "knowledge within oneself." Acting in good conscience means acting upon a sense of what needs to be done. To follow one's conscience means being faithful to the inner voice. Freedom of conscience is the bedrock of our lives because conscience frees us to make decisions that are faithful to who we are.

Catholic tradition affirms that the primacy of individual conscience must always be honored. As Germain Grisez writes, "one must follow one's conscience even when it is mistaken ... since it is one's last and best judgment as to what one should choose."[26] Following one's conscience does not mean ignoring voices other than one's own or not being open to change. The wisdom gained from personal experience, current findings from psychological and social sciences, the beautiful inputs of the arts, the values we uphold and the spiritual teachings we believe in (for example, those revealed through the gospels and the church), can all help us nurture or inform our conscience. Human beings are not isolated islands; we grow through interaction and dialogue with community, which can include our families, our group of friends, our teachers, and our churches. Even within community, however, as much as we listen to others and ponder their input, we cannot abdicate the responsibility to decide for ourselves what makes sense by listening to our personal consciences.

Any community that does not respect the individual's freedom becomes a cult. A community should encourage its members to listen to their inner voice and not suppress it with the excuse of blind obedience. If deep inside Katie "just knew" that she needed to live in another residential context instead of L'Arche, her community needed to trust her and empower her to follow that inner voice, not have her stay at all costs. We encouraged her to listen to her loved ones and take into account the information she gathered on her options, but we trusted her to make her own decision, even if the decision would have made some people unhappy.

When people follow their conscience, they might meet resistance from family members, friends or even authority figures. Nevertheless, people should follow that "knowledge within." During the Cold War era of the 1950s, Dorothy Day, the pacifist founder of the Catholic Worker movement for social justice, was arrested three times for refusing to participate in civil defense drills in New York City. For her, participating in the drills meant complying with preparations for nuclear war, which she resisted. Dorothy disobeyed the law and civic authorities tried to compel her to obey, but she remained faithful to herself. In a letter to the Duke of Norfolk, John Henry Newman quotes the Spanish Franciscan Antonio Corduba's reflection that "in no manner is it lawful to act against conscience, even though a Law, or a Superior commands it."[27] Individual conscience bears the highest authority in making life decisions.

The term that names the decision-making process while listening to one's conscience is "discernment," from the Latin *discernere*, to separate and distinguish. Although Katie was firm in wanting to move out of L'Arche, she was encouraged, as part of her decision-making, to ponder the pros and cons of that idea, distinguishing between the excitement for newness and the long-term ramifications of taking such an action. Katie also needed to distinguish her voice from that of her parents, who preferred that she not move. Her parents were not her legal guardians, thus not having the responsibility of making decisions for her (even if they were, they would hopefully still take into account Katie's preferences). Ultimately, in making her decision, Katie needed to separate the voice of her conscience from any other voice, listening to it and trusting it.

Since L'Arche is a faith community, many of its members invite God into their decision-making. Conscience is our own inner voice, which can communicate with God's voice. In a love relationship, partners dialogue but don't force the other to think or act in a certain way. Similarly, God respects our conscience and freedom as a lover would his or her beloved. A scripture passage portrays God standing at the door of our hearts knocking: "Listen! I am standing at the door, knocking; if you hear my voice and open the door, I will come in to you and eat with you, and you with me" (Rev 3:20).

God's voice, a loving voice, encourages us to get in touch with our own inner voice. Because we are created in God's image and likeness, our profound being and fundamental desires are willed by God. In the Gospel of Mark Jesus asks a blind man, "What do you want me to do for you?" (Mk 10:51). He asks him what his desire was, where his need lay. Jesus could have said, "I know what you want," but he is respectful; he asked and empowered him to find within himself what he really wanted. The Gospel of John narrates a similar scene. One day while walking, Jesus turns to see two disciples of John the Baptist following him. He asks, "What are you looking for?" (Jn 1:38). Jesus invites these two individuals to heed their own inner voice and desire. He didn't tell them what they were looking for; he asked them and wanted them to ponder their answer. If, therefore, we ask what God wants as we make decisions, we may need to be ready to receive the same question back—what is it that we want? In this case, discernment is a conversation. Sedlak writes, "Instead of a God with a well-mapped-out plan that we have to 'discern,' we have a God who invites us to participate in creating the plan itself, a shared future."[28]

We are created for love and that is what ultimately matters; in the words of Augustine, "Love, and do what thou wilt."[29] When we make decisions, therefore, one way by which we can guide our discernment and heed our conscience is noticing whether a specific idea, option, or experience brings consolation or desolation. Healing ministry practitioners Matthew, Sheila, and Dennis Linn have framed consolation as anything that helps us receive and give love, and desolation as whatever blocks our capacity to receive and give love.[30] We live love in personal and unique ways, so our decisions are deeply subjective. Like good musicians improvising together, human beings are invited to enter freely into the theme of God's saving love in ways that are "genuinely unpredictable, free and novel,"[31] as John R. Sachs writes. When we sense and generate ways of living out our being that "fit" and bring us to a more loving place (not all do), it is likely that we are in touch with our inner voice and are being faithful to it.

Believing in ourselves means taking responsibility for our lives, becoming aware of what gives us life and taking responsibility for our choices, trusting and following our inner voice, our conscience. When we make decisions according to conscience we witness to the importance of our personal experience and become protagonists of our lives, tracing our unique way of being in the world.

Believing in the Other

Encountering the Other

No person comes out of nowhere, nor are our lives possible without relationships. Believing in ourselves can put us in touch with our basic thirst for relationship and incites us to encounter others and recognize that, in our similarities and differences, in our capacities and needs, we share a common humanity that encourages us to be in community.

The joy of the encounter and the power of relationship is something that Albert, a core member with gifts of welcome and friendliness, knows quite well. Albert and I were once housemates in L'Arche; our mutual encounter developed over some months. When I first started living in his home, as a new assistant, we were strangers. It took weeks to get to know one other, becoming familiar with our ways of being and of doing things while establishing bonds of trust. Although some people enter community wanting to establish relationships right away and to know people as much as possible quickly, this can evoke the opposite result. Of course, there can be excitement in getting to know people, but it also takes time to build trust and develop a friendship.

During my first days of knowing Albert, I found his speech difficult to understand. He had an impediment that I was not used to, so I needed time to learn his language and his way of communicating. He probably needed time to learn my language as well, including getting accustomed to my Italian accent. All those thick vowels and that fluctuating cadence!

On first impression Albert seemed friendly and quick to laughter. He was pretty laid back, enjoying sporting events on television in the evening and retreating to his room to write in solitude once home from work. Living with him, however, allowed me to encounter him at a level deeper than what first impressions conveyed. Albert was a sensitive man, thirsting for relationship. He sometimes got quite sad when assistants to whom he had grown close moved out of his house. Seeing them leave was hard. Albert would release his disappointment by crying out his pain, sobbing and screaming, at times blasting out highly emotional love songs on the stereo to accompany his emotional outburst. Albert's anguish was related to the loss of people to whom he had grown close but had left. I came to know Albert's outgoing and friendly side, as well as his melancholy and sorrow. Our relationship deepened through many other encounters and turned into a friendship.

I have not forgotten how, one evening, Albert affirmed the beauty and importance of relationship through a simple question. I had just returned to the community home after a vacation. I entered the house with my jacket and luggage at hand and went into the kitchen. Albert welcomed me back by giving me a big hug. After the hug he looked directly in my eyes and asked, with his deep and raspy voice, "Did you miss me?"

That question, "Did you miss me?" was both touching and profoundly revelatory. Albert was asking if I missed him while I was gone, if his absence made itself felt while I was away, if his friendship still had a place in my heart even if I was in another state. Albert's inquiry, however, was a profoundly human question most of us might have never dared to ask. We tell people we haven't seen in a long time, "I have missed you." However, we have probably never had the courage to ask them, as Albert did, "Did you miss me?" Why? What is it that blocks us from asking such an unfiltered question from the heart?

In public discourse, individualism is often elevated over community, independence over interdependence, and self-assured reasoning over emotional sharing. Those very realities, encouraged and rewarded, run the danger of locking us inside our individual selves. Albert's words, however, invite us to move beyond our isolation and pretenses of self-reliance, and live from that place in our hearts where we desire to love and to be loved. This is the place from which we reach out for relationship and seek to encounter others and form community, letting them know they are not alone, that we share life with them. This is the place in our lives where people are important and are missed if they are not there (and we are missed if we are not in theirs).

Without over-sentimentalizing relationship, it is a basis of everything that we are. From its origin our very being is shaped by relationship. A brief look at human development, from conception to death, testifies to this.

We were born from the intimate encounter between our parents, outside our control, totally dependent on them. After conception, our mother's body maintained us; after birth we needed parental security, acceptance, and protection. Many children gradually develop anxiety upon moments of separation from parents, realizing they are their own beings.

During childhood, the way people treated us —lovingly, aggressively, or neglectfully—influenced our understanding of ourselves, God, and the world. As a result, we may have grown with a healthy self-esteem and curiosity towards others or with a sense of inferiority and abjection.

As children, we looked for friends with whom to play and discover the world, and for spaces where we could develop our gifts and interests. Our relationship with people, nature, and things developed through wonder, learning, and risk. During those years, a spirituality of unity with creation, untainted by over-thinking, followed our every step without us realizing it.

During adolescence, we became more concerned with others' perceptions of us, the way we presented ourselves to them, and how we identified as individuals and as members of a group, particularly as we noticed changes in our bodies and in our way of seeing things. Around that time, the relational world of dating likely began to open us to the beauty of first love and to the pain of heartbreak.

As we grow into adulthood, we make major life decisions and events, potentially giving ourselves to others through marriage, a consecrated life, or a single life in community. Some of us have kids, feeling the joy of bringing another person into the world, but also feeling pain when those children grow and leave the home. Some develop a sense of responsibility towards self and others through socially meaningful work or service.

In old age people find themselves enjoying grandchildren or sharing a lifetime of wisdom, but they also experience the pain of loss (of health, of memory, of loved ones), ultimately approaching death, a mysterious and dark end to earthly relationships. But it also carries the sparkle of a passage towards eternity in loving communion with one another and with God.

Relationships are crucial to our being; nevertheless, many flee them or put up barriers that block deep and rich encounters. They may fear vulnerability, feel embarrassed at their dependence, or have been hurt in the past and don't quite know how to recover trust in others. Living with people who have intellectual disabilities has helped me appreciate our interdependence and the value of community, built on admitting our need for others and sharing our common humanity.

Although the two words are sometimes used interchangeably, encountering others does not mean merely meeting them, which is only a first step. Encounter moves beyond meeting. In an encounter we engage with someone from within, we get to know them while respecting the mystery that they are and we allow for the possibility of mutual transformation. We put our lives in touch with theirs. In his *I and Thou*, Martin Buber focuses on how people relate.[32] Buber differentiates two distinct modes of engaging: "I-It" and "I-Thou." In the first mode, "I-It," we relate to others and to the world as a collection of things to be experienced—known, understood, and analyzed. We therefore turn the other into an "it," an object that can fit into our experience and comprehension. In the second mode, "I-Thou," we encounter and relate to others as they are—in what we see and what we can't see, what we understand and what we can't understand—open to being transformed in the process.

The "I-It" mode of relating is quite common. It happens anytime we look at people in a way that seeks to "grasp" who they are. In doing so, we reduce them to what we can know. When we talk about others only in terms of being liberals or conservatives, straights or gays, seculars or religious, good guys or enemies, we risk turning them into an "it." In other words, we use our understanding of some of their characteristics (personal, social, political, religious) to identify the whole person. It is easy to slip into doing this. Since not knowing can create anxiety, we facilely divide the world into categories.

Instead, in the "I-Thou" mode (or the "being-to-being" mode of relating), we approach others as unique entities without reducing them to categories of understanding or seeking to control them. Although when used well words can help describe a person, people's mystery is too great to be contained by them. An encounter with other people, including those from different cultural, political, or religious backgrounds, can open up vistas that are exciting to discover and learn from. Such an encounter can leave us different than how we were before experiencing it. When I met Albert, for example, I took time to learn his language and his ways, but I also looked at him as a mystery I couldn't fully comprehend. There are many things we don't know about who we are and contemplating that allows us to accept people as they are without needing to wrap our minds around them.

By moving from an "I-It" to an "I-Thou" mode of relating, we form community. In my own community leadership, for example, during new assistants' orientation and formation, I sought to encourage assistants to discover for themselves who their housemates were, providing some information about them already early on but "just enough" of it, not wanting them to reduce those individuals to a list of characteristics or qualities. Whenever new assistants are too eager to learn about other community members, wanting to know and understand right away their communication styles, their favorite things to do, and their challenging behaviors, they are likely coming from an "I-It" impulse.

Through an "I-Thou" encounter, we can welcome that the other is different from ourselves in ways that we don't always understand, but also that we share a common human state with them. When people know of my work with individuals that have disabilities they compliment me for "helping the needy" or "helping the poor." But this framing of people with disabilities as "the needy" is often a way to distance them, de-personalize them, and highlight how different they are from the "average person," rather than to recognize how we are all needy and we are all poor, in the sense that we all have a need we seek to satisfy or a lack we seek to fill. That comes with being human. This is not to deny that some people can have clear and obvious needs that others may not have—someone who can't walk may need a wheelchair; someone who can't see may need a cane, and someone who can't feed himself might need assistance in eating. However, at our core, we all share elemental needs that generally go unnoticed as they are met. We all need food to survive, but since in richer countries that is so easily obtained we don't "see" how disabling not having food can be. We all need clothes and shelter from severe weather, but because they are commonly provided we don't feel how deadly it can be not to have those resources. We all need a listening ear, a shoulder to lean on, an encouraging word, someone to be quiet with, someone who can help us reach our potential. Some view people with unusual or visible impairments as "exotic," not realizing that we all share the same principal human needs, whether we have disabilities or not.

Besides what we all lack and need, we also share wonderful human capacities. We all have a capacity to love and to be present to others, once again whether we have disabilities or not. We may demonstrate this capacity by giving attention, empowering those who feel down, sharing in solidarity from our strengths and brokenness, or simply by letting others know that they were missed when not around, as Albert did with me.

A culture built around the beauty of the encounter and our basic human desire for relationship is a culture of community. A culture not built around encounter and relationship quickly turns inhumane, without focus. Whenever money, corrupt interests, unbridled power, or idealized notions of the human person become the center of our social structure we all suffer. Society then becomes a harsh competition to be the richest, smartest, prettiest, and quickest, in turn marginalizing and oppressing those that don't fit those categories.

Our society needs community, and our history as a species points to this. I'd like to note here a fascinating archeological finding from the 1950s, in modern-day Iraq. It challenges our tendency to define the development of our species as a "survival of the fittest," in which only the strongest or most powerful are successful. Archeologists discovered tombs in which Neanderthal people had apparently been buried on beds of flowers. One of the skeletons, found by Ralph Solecki, was that of Shanidar I, a man about forty-years-old who must have lived a profoundly impaired life: he was partially blind and had a severed arm, and, because of these impairments, could not have hunted and provided for himself. People were there for him. He could not have survived without care and sustenance. This is a testament to Neanderthal humanity and compassion, as expressed by paleontologists Erik Trinkaus and Pat Shipman in their summary of Solecki's findings.[33] Later discoveries confirmed that, in those early years of our species, this man's story was not an exception.[34] We have reason to believe that our ancestors were not uncaring stereotypical primitive brutes using physical strength to survive at all costs. They could be supportive and relational, caring for people's needs and creating community. We daresay that, at a deep level, our human ancestry is one of survival through community rather than only one of survival of the fittest.

One of our fundamental human needs and human capacities is for relationship—encountering others and entering into relationship with them. Although the other person is always a mystery that cannot be fully understood, when we encounter them we realize our common humanity, composed of similarities and differences, capacities and needs. By sharing these very human life realities with one another, we form community.

Being with the Other

We become a community when we enter into relationship and, in some way, share our lives with others. One way to share life is by engaging in activities that bond us together and build relationship. Even in teams, as at work or in sports, however, we may experience a sense of togetherness around a shared cause without necessarily sensing that our lives belong together. A foundational way to share life in community, which goes beyond (but can include) doing things together, is the ability to be present to the other and to their lives. When we are present to them we can reveal that we are close to them and cherish them not for what they do, how they perform, or what they believe in, but simply because they are who they are.

Communities can take different shapes and forms. We can create community with a small number of people or with a larger group. We can build community with loved ones or with people we barely know. We can come together as a community around a mission or just because we share a specific interest. We can belong to communities founded on diverse values. We can be part of a community for a long time or for a short period. We can even form community virtually, as people around the world with similar interests and values have the opportunity of sharing these remotely. In any case, a community is a group of people that share life and grow together through that life, whatever appearance it may have.

In L'Arche there are two ways of "being with" in community that I particularly enjoy, namely the activity of sharing a meal and the non-activity of quietly sitting together. Each evening, at a consistent time, the home gathers around the dining room table, set up for the occasion. This is a most important aspect of life together: no matter where community members have been during the day and what their commitments were, they can count on being together for the evening meal.

Dinner is usually prepared by an assistant and a core member, as is setting the table. Preparing a good meal and presenting an aesthetically pleasing dinner set-up imply a tasteful intentionality to share and be together, showing that each person has a place at the table, that their presence is valued and that they are being well taken care of. Jennifer, for example, enjoys preparing pizza and groups different toppings in separate colored bowls so that people can add their own favorite extras as they wish. She takes care of people by providing food that meets their taste and preferences.

At the end of the meal, each person helps clear the table. Dishes and cups are brought from the dining room to the kitchen, and placemats are put back in the drawer. One of the assistants washes the dishes in the sink or, helped by a core member, puts them in the dishwasher. As the evening progresses, the sound of rinsing and cleaning gives way to a deep silence. Once the kitchen is clean and orderly, in fact, everyone sits again at the table, now stripped of dinner decor but with a candle positioned in the middle for prayer time. The lights are turned off and the lit candle is passed around, inviting people to rest in silence, vocally or silently offering their prayers if they so desire. Some take a deep breath to let go of the cares of the day and to center themselves. Others look around. Some keep their eyes closed, while others look at the flame's slow movement. In that quiet atmosphere, there reigns a sensation of moving beyond self to open the space to someone bigger, who can be trusted with our needs, joys, and concerns. At the end of prayer, each person gets up and embarks on whatever they might have in mind for the rest of the evening—watching a movie, coloring, calling parents and friends, or going directly to bed.

Around the table, dinner-time can be one of the most important ways of nourishing life in a community - physically through the food that sustains individuals, emotionally through conversational sharing, and spiritually through appreciation of the meal and God's presence as it takes place. The meal can be an important sign of encounter and community.

Not only can the act of cooking express love to others, but around the table, amid our diversity, we are all equal. Whether we have great intellectual abilities or profound intellectual disabilities, whether we eat with a fork or with a tube, whether our bodies are skinny or chubby, whether we are black or white, whether we are rich or poor, whether we are religious or not, we all need to be fed. Eating brings unity—we can all share and take delight in it.

The enjoyment of supper is typically accompanied by people commenting on their day, light or substantial conversations, recollections, moments of laughter, but sometimes also sparks of tension, depending on each person's mood. People are invited to come to the table as they are. The communication and exchanges over a meal help us to get to know one another better and be present to each other. Engaging with people, listening to them, and allowing them to express themselves, states that they have a place not only at the table, but also in our lives.

Besides the conviviality of communal meal-time, I also enjoy being present to people without doing much, possibly even enjoying some silence with them, as when Jacob and I, during sharing time, sat in the living room without saying much, went on walks around the neighborhood, or played cards, sometimes chatting, sometimes laughing, sometimes singing Tina Turner tunes, but also remaining quiet.

Jacob is no stranger to silence and its value in community life. A storyteller and improv musician, Jacob also makes sure to safeguard his daily spaces for silence. He likes to be in the house when, as he puts it, there is "peace and quiet." He often sits in the living room for prolonged times to write letters on his notepad—full pages of As, Bs, Cs … He consistently takes the house dog out for quiet walks around the neighborhood as the evening falls, and he enjoys sitting on the porch when the weather is warm, at times with a beer at hand, simply observing what is around him.

Unlike Jacob, another core member, Leo, cannot talk, sit, walk, or feed himself. He has quadriplegia. When I lived with

Leo, we shared silence of a different quality than the one I share with Jacob. Jacob, even after a long silence, could express himself verbally if he so desired; Leo didn't. At times, to engage with Leo, I or another housemate would turn on his favorite music (polka songs) and we would hold his hands and move them to the rhythm of the music, a spontaneous and happy dance. Leo would emit sounds of joy. I would usually share time with Leo by his wheelchair, looking him in the eyes or just sitting next to him—being present to him. Our moments together were not about being productive, but they were fruitful, since our relationship was nurtured in that quiet "being with." There is a difference between productivity (doing and creating things) and fruitfulness (being life-giving), as the latter can happen without any specific end in mind, whatever our abilities and disabilities. I can't deny, however, how hard it was, if not impossible, to know what Leo was thinking, even if some communication was mysteriously being exchanged in our shared silences.

Some people might be uncomfortable with silence, but its benefits ought not be underestimated. When people cannot find stillness of being within themselves, their lives easily become scattered, hectic, dispersed, noisy—and consequently so do their relationships. Blaise Pascal believed that the unhappiness of humankind arose from our inability to stay quietly in our own room.[35] "Room" can be taken to represent one's inner center or literally a physical space. A story is told of a monk in the Egyptian desert who traveled a long way to see an elder and ask him for a good word. Having arrived at the destination, the elder encouraged him to return where he came from, telling him: "Go, sit in your cell, and your cell will teach you everything."[36] If we don't take quiet time to be present to ourselves our relationships quickly become an escape from facing our reality, or they become an attachment to others because we are not touch with ourselves.

Silence is necessary but should not be over-idealized. Although silence can hold great meaning, between people there can also be angry silences, careless silences, neglectful silences and frustrating silences. Some people might want to communicate but they cannot, and silence becomes like a wall. Silence is not a "one-size-fits-all" realm.

On a crisp spring day years ago, I went on a pilgrimage with other community members to the French Alps. When we reached the Chartreuse Mountains, the sun was shining and the air was fresh. As we walked the stony streets we could feel stillness in the air and hear the echo of our steps. We chatted and we stayed silent, we laughed at our jokes and we remained quiet as we heard the trickle of a small fountain, we looked at each other and we admired the green grandeur of the robust forest on the mountaintops. Through our words we felt close to each other; through our silences we gave each other space. Choosing when to exchange words and when to remain silent was like a dance, which could only be discovered in relationship.

Language has undeniable power. We reveal ourselves through verbal communication and gestures, giving words and shape to our experiences, so that we can share part of our lives. By naming our experiences and ideas, but also our subjective feelings (even if others have the same ideas as we do, nobody feels the same way about them as we do), we can let people know who we really are and become vulnerable to them. Thanks to language we can tap in the bonding and therapeutic potential of talking and self-revelation, as well as access the artistic bounty of poetic, literary, and lyrical expression. In my relationship with Jacob, as much as he and I are fine being together quietly (in the same room, walking together or during a video call), we also both like to talk about life (I am a conversationalist and he likes to share), and he is often eager to speak words of wisdom during simple and ordinary moments.

Not filling space with too many words, however, can help each of us inhabit reality when language fails. As life-giving as verbal communication can be, we might appreciate those friends that just "get us" or can be with us comfortably even when we don't have much, if anything, to say. Nouwen wisely noted that, "When we honestly ask ourselves which persons in our lives mean the most to us, we often find that it is those who, instead of giving much advice, solutions, or cures, have chosen rather to share our pain and touch our wounds with a gentle and tender hand. The friend who can be silent with us in a moment of despair or confusion, who can stay with us in an hour of grief and bereavement, who can tolerate not-knowing, not-curing, not-healing, and face with us the reality of our powerlessness, that is the friend who cares."[37]

There is a limit to what words can convey. Although words can communicate and reveal, they can also conceal our true experience. Words can fail to convey the depth of what we live. How often have we found ourselves trying to share a memory or describe how we are doing and not finding the words to do so. "I am struggling to find the right word" or "There are just no words for it," we might answer in such circumstances. Italo Calvino tackles this by imagining Venetian explorer Marco Polo trying to describe the cities he has traveled to and ultimately saying, "Memory's images, once they are fixed in words, are erased. Perhaps I am afraid of losing Venice all at once, if I speak of it. Or perhaps, speaking of other cities, I have already lost it, little by little."[38] Calvino conveys, with poetic exaggeration, how in the moment we take the breadth of our experience and squeeze it into a few words, we "change it," constricting it into language that cannot contain it. Silence, on the other hand, can help us find out that many things which can't be fully captured in words can be held together in silence.

Believing in ourselves, as we have seen earlier, implies letting ourselves be and breathe freely, rather than filling up every moment with anxious activity in an effort to construct ourselves. In a similar way, relating to people and forming community with them is built on the simplicity of being with them, whether through activity or inactivity, through words or silence.

Meeting the Other at the Margins

It is easy to be drawn towards people similar to us, rather those different from us. When we surround ourselves with people that think like us, look like us and live like us we remain within our comfort zones and our hearts don't stretch beyond them. In so doing, however, our fear of others risks growing proportionally. The more we close ourselves in our group, the more we tend to feel threatened by those outside of it. Fear can then become a lonely space we inhabit and live from, which we neither question nor challenge. Sufi poet Hafiz describes fear as "the cheapest room in the house. I would like to see you living in better conditions …"[39] If we want to grow in trust beyond our fears, in some way we need to leave the "cheapest room in the house" and go onto the margins, to meet the other that is different from us.

When I first joined L'Arche my outlook was in some ways a bit simplistic and rigid. Although I have always been quite sensitive to the human spirit, during part of my young adult years I approached truth—about self, God, and society—in relatively stark "black and white" terms. I was taught that if I believed certain things then truth was on my side, and as an idealistic young adult I didn't question that perspective. Community helped me grow out of this phase and encouraged me to make more space for the reality in front of me and the truth in it. As I encountered people from multiple lifestyles, different cultures, various belief systems, and diverse outlooks (even from within my own faith tradition!), my vision was gradually softened and deepened as I got to relate with them, hear their questions, learn from their experience and reflect on their words. At first this was hard, as meeting people who challenge your beliefs and feeling that you have to defend "the truth" makes relationships energy-consuming and conflictual. With time, however, I have learned that we are all searching for truth and that others' genuine seeking and journeying deserve the same respect and grace as mine.

This transformation happened not only as I approached people and their ideas from a deeper level, but also as I related to myself differently. I discovered that if I was rigid with others' ideas, I was also with mine. Engaging in experience, encounter, and reflection, particularly with people who have been marginalized, and paying attention to the areas within myself that I marginalized, has transformed how I see and understand myself, God, and others.

Before talking about going to the margins and meeting others, we need to start with encountering the "marginalized other" within ourselves, since we often project the dynamics that we experience within ourselves onto the external world. Psychoanalysis has explored two levels of our mental lives: the conscious, which relates to the aware and thinking mind, and the unconscious, which is the psyche's reservoir of memories, feelings, and thoughts beyond our conscious awareness. We often relegate to the unconscious that which we do not wish to see in ourselves. If we have an idealized image of ourselves as helper, truth-bearer, successful person, or loving savior, we might reject and repress those elements within ourselves that do not meet those ideas. For instance, people who see themselves as "the helpers" may recognize an honorable part of their personality (that which helps others) but may also disregard the contradictory parts within themselves that do not wish to help others or the fact that they may be neglecting themselves by focusing only on others. Similarly, if people have ideas or urges that they'd rather not have, they may deny and suppress them, instead of recognizing them and deciding to move forward faithful to what they value. The "out of sight, out of mind" approach does not work well. Although we may keep unwanted mental contents at bay, out of our immediate awareness, they do add up in our unconscious. For this reason, the unconscious is sometimes identified as our shadow side: as we marginalize to the outskirts of our psyche that which we'd rather not admit about ourselves and others, we press into mental storage a lot of content and energy, which remains alive, influencing our thinking and behaviors without us even realizing it.

Going to the margins of our psyche helps us grow in self-awareness, allowing us to acknowledge what we find there and live in a more unified way. Our shadow side may contain the root of our fears, compulsions, and obsessions. It can hide painful memories, unsettling emotions, and confusing thoughts. Accepting these, of course, doesn't mean uncovering everything at once, which could be overly destabilizing, nor acting out on whatever pops up in the recesses of our psychic life. It does mean becoming comfortable with our human complexity, nuances, and paradoxes, which can provide us with wisdom for our human development. Teresa of Avila emphasizes the importance of self-knowledge, "so important that, even if you were raised right up to the heavens, I should like you never to relax your cultivation of it."[40]

Recognizing that within ourselves, alongside energies of love and peace-making, there are forces of division and fear, grounded in experiences and memories, can help us move forward with greater freedom. At a meeting with L'Arche assistants someone once compared being part of community to being part of a family, so as to highlight the positive and consoling nature of living together. One assistant responded that such an image can be unhelpful for those who might have had a damaging experience of family. For them, hearing that joining community resembles in any way being part of a family could be triggering, since they equate family with dysfunction. Learning to recognize how our memories may affect us while also freeing ourselves from their negative influence takes time, patience, and support.

Befriending our shadow is not only a step for psychological well-being, but also a spiritual one. Anselm Gruen mentions how "the way to God leads through the encounter with myself, through the descent into my reality,"[41] echoing the words of desert father Evagrius Ponticus: "You want to know God? First know yourself."[42] Our internal images and experiences shape our image of God. William G. Justice and Warren Lambert have found, for example, that those who have had negative experiences with their parents have a more negative concept of the personality of God.[43] They may project onto God the anger or violence they may have experienced with their parents, without even realizing it! Such images of God need to be healed. For instance, those who perceive God as a vengeful father rather than a loving one might be basing their understanding on punishment experienced at the hand of their earthly fathers during their upbringing, which now unconsciously influences how they see God. They might also have been spiritually abused by people pushing that unhealthy image of God on them.[44] On the other hand, people who have had positive loving experiences during their upbringing might more readily understand the unconditional love of God, who, as the Linns point out, "loves us, just for a start, at least as much as the person who loves us the most,"[45] but also goes infinitely beyond.

Our unconscious also influences how we relate to ourselves and others. People who judge and condemn those different than they are may be judging and condemning aspects of their own selves that they'd rather not acknowledge. They keep "the strangers" outside of their circles, even making them into a threatening enemy, so that they don't have to deal with their own inner reality. Out of fear and whatever else feeds it (imaginary or not), they can cause social tension and conflict, building different kinds of walls that create distance and separation between individuals and groups. For example, if someone judges people with drug addictions as mere "irresponsible ones" with too much time on their hands, they may not have recognized within themselves the potential to be addicted to something (alcohol, money, power, influence, emotional dependency, religious fundamentalism, ideology and so forth). They may think of themselves as different than "them," but in actuality they may not be as different as they'd like to think.

The divisions that separate individuals, groups and societies can seem insurmountable. Nonetheless, each person can cross over the wall between "us" and "them" in their own ways. This could mean reflecting on who we have relegated to the margins of our lives (maybe, someone against whom we hold a grudge, someone that we find annoying or someone that has hurt us) and seeing if we can make peace, or at least forgive them if they have wronged us. It could also mean meeting someone from a different demographic or cultural group and listen to their story. Core members Francis and Jacob, with assistant Andrea, for example, have crossed a wall in making it a point to visit a retirement house on their weekends, to meet and engage with the elderly, a population marginalized by a culture that emphasizes speed and efficiency.

In the New Testament, Jesus asks people to invite, over a meal, the poor, the crippled, the lame, and the blind, rather than their friends, relatives, and wealthy neighbors that can repay them (Lk 14:12-14). In so doing he encourages them to form communities of diversity, with a particular eye towards those that are poor and isolated, what the church's social theology has called a "preferential option for the poor."

It is enriching to create diverse and inclusive spaces where people can meet. For an event I organized some time ago, I invited Ada, a Muslim member of L'Arche, to share how her Islamic faith informed and is in turn influenced by her community involvement. She shared how she interpreted the latter in terms of the pillars of Islam, and attendees were glad to hear this voice that they had not heard before. Ada was from a minority group and I wanted her to be heard, even if most other community members had different religious backgrounds; it was good to learn how she interpreted our shared life according to her personal beliefs and how she too, similarly to others, found meaning and richness in community with people with disabilities.

Simone de Beauvoir believed that our being human is more important than the peculiarities that distinguish us.[46] By encountering one another and letting down the barriers and blocks between us, we can embark together on a journey of trust in the midst of our differences, following a path of unity grounded in our shared humanity.

Celebrating the Other

The people we encounter have had their joys and pains, their ups and downs. They may hold excitement and happiness, as well as sorrow and fatigue. People may carry lightness and serenity, as well as hardships and struggles. Even if we don't know what they are going through, approaching them from a place of benevolence can help them know that they are valued and that, wherever they are in their life journey, their life is important. The wisdom of gentleness leads us to treat people with care, to approach humanity with reverence. The spirituality of gentleness can help us connect our kindness also to the recognition that the other is precious and important in God's eyes.

As we recognize the beauty and potential of others, while listening and seeking to understand where they come from, we show that we believe in them. We affirm the gift they bring to the world and celebrate them as they are. This can help them feel that they belong, empowering them to grow with the knowledge that they are loved.

One of the most celebrating people I have ever met is David, a core member whom I have known for a few years. David is amicable and cheerful, very perceptive and observant of people's moods. Although he has challenges communicating verbally, his body language can be very expressive. For example, if David is happy to be at an event, he picks a front seat to be an active and attentive participant. If, on the other hand, he has other things on his mind and is not excited to be there, his expression can turn serious and his gaze pensive.

David loves people, and when he is around someone he is happy to see he zooms in on them and expresses his joy in seeing them by giving friendly handshakes, big hugs, and sometimes kisses. Assistants periodically need to remind him to kiss others on the cheek, rather than aim for other parts of people's faces.

David is a man of great hospitality. When I had dinner or set up the space for gatherings at David's community home,

I often found him sitting at the dining room table ready to have supper. As soon as he saw me, David jumped up from his chair to give me a big hug and to greet me. He does this with various people in community that come through the door. David runs out of his way to greet them and to embrace them, no questions asked, with a big smile and making joyful sounds.

David actively participates in a monthly gathering where assistants and core members celebrate their anniversaries. As part of these get-togethers, community members sit in a semi-circle and share affirmations with each person being celebrated. These affirmations, usually spoken but at times drawn or written down, validate the person's gifts, talents, and qualities. When we affirm someone, we highlight what we like about their personality, mention the good things they bring into our lives, and remember precious moments shared. When the moment for affirmations during anniversary celebrations begins, David is the first to share. He ensures his chair is positioned in front of the person to affirm and speaks his appreciative words to them. David likes affirming others so much that even during ordinary dinners he spontaneously affirms his housemates around the table one-by-one, often telling them what good friends they have been to him. He then even asks them to affirm him in return!

David lets people know that they are appreciated, that he enjoys seeing them and that they are welcomed as they are. Sometimes people come to the house in which David lives tired, upset at somebody, or with worries. They may feel insecure or anxious. David does not analyze them, accuse them, nor does he ignore them. He gives them a hug, reserves a space at the table for them, and affirms them with a smile. He conveys that they are noticed and loved, that they can bring a smile to someone's life.

David's celebratory embrace of others is similar to God's, whose unconditional love is expressed in the parable of the lost son. In the story, a father sees his son return after having left for a far-away country where he wasn't doing well and where he lost his money. While he was still far away, "his father saw him and was filled with compassion; he ran and put his arms around him and kissed him" (Lk 15:20). The father did not ask any questions; he ran to embrace him lovingly and to welcome him home, happy to be together and calling for a celebration to be made in his honor.

People can be so caught up in personal concerns, insecurities, and life challenges that they forget the beauty they carry within them, the gift they bring to the world and the potential they hold. When we notice these and affirm them accordingly, we remind people of who they are. We let them know that it is good to be together, that the world is better because they are with us. Practicing affirmation also encourages us to find the good in others, even if they get on our nerves or we take their presence for granted. An inspiring story involving the mystic, Thomas Merton speaks of finding light in others. Merton narrates how one day, while in a shopping district, he was awakened to the splendor of others:

> In Louisville, at the corner of Fourth and Walnut, in the center of the shopping district, I was suddenly overwhelmed with the realization that I loved all those people, that they were mine and I theirs, that we could not be alien to one another even though we were total strangers ... I have the immense joy of being man, a member of a race in which God Himself became incarnate. As if the sorrows and stupidities of the human condition could overwhelm me, now I realize what we all are. And if only everybody could realize this! But it cannot be explained. There is no way of telling people that they are all walking around shining like the sun.[47]

Although such an experience may appear quite grand, it is simple, spontaneous, and effortless. One can imagine being in a shopping district (or any other everyday setting where we live our lives) and suddenly feel a sense of appreciation towards the people around us. When we allow whatever it is that we appreciate about them emerge within us and express this to them, we are bringing celebration right into our ordinary lives.

To avoid misunderstandings, appreciation must be realistic, not puffed-up flattery. Celebrating someone does not mean denying aspects of their person we find challenging or even upsetting, nor does it mean pretending that they are "perfect" (who is?). As a matter of fact, building community does not happen only through celebration but also through forgiveness—and the constant interplay of the two. Being upset at someone and jumping too quickly into celebrating might feel strident, as it doesn't consider the time needed to forgive the other person, freeing ourselves from the power of what they might have done to us and approaching them somewhat renewed. Celebrating does, however, help them—and us—remember that somewhere in their core there is a light. Celebration also highlights and makes space for their gifts, which make the world a better place. If someone is a good listener, a good cook, a practical thinker, or a talented musician, without being given the opportunities to listen, cook, solve problems, or play music, then being celebrated for those gifts sounds hollow and divorced from reality. Celebration therefore not only touches the individual, but it brings about social change, as people's gifts are valued and given space to grow.

When people recognize that their gifts make a difference in other people's lives, they can feel more motivated to develop them and to share them with new people. A community that celebrates, therefore, is not meant to be a flattering relational space that is insular or closed in itself, as it happens in cults that use emotional manipulation to keep people in their suffocating circles. Community should rather affirm people so that they can live their gifts freely, with freedom of growth, exploration of life and being a blessing to other people's lives!

I once met Monica, a woman with an intellectual disability, who likes to take a lot of pictures: of people, of places, of objects. In reflecting on her interest in taking pictures and keeping them, I am reminded, in some way, of celebration. Although some might have difficulty in expressing appreciation and affirmation in words, they may still express them in their own ways through action. Monica's photo-taking might be a way for her to say that she appreciates the people in her life, the places she visits, and the objects she comes across, so much so that she wants to "encapsulate" the memory of them in images - to look at, to cherish, to celebrate.

Celebration, in its various forms, can be directed at a person but also at a group. Celebration has a one-to-one dynamic, as in the example of David individually affirming each of his housemates around the dinner table. This way of celebrating is essential because it is person-centered: the other person is valued not in generalized terms but in their singularity. Celebrating others, however, can also be centered on a group of people or a culture. On a yearly basis, for example, I and other L'Arche members took part in disability pride parades to celebrate disability culture. During these parades, people with disabilities march alongside their allies and friends to celebrate who they are, proclaiming that they are proud of their identity and advocating for recognition of their rights. Considering their history as an oppressed minority group that has had its basic human rights trampled upon, this celebration can help bring about far-ranging social and political change.

If celebrations are often joyous and lively occasions, in which the people present can smile, relax and lighten up, they can also happen amid sorrow and tears. When friends move away, when kids grow up and leave home, or, even more drastically, when someone we love passes away, celebrating them can feel like lighting a little light while being surrounded by darkness.

Francis was a core member whose unexpected death upset community, but whose spirit is still being celebrated. He was a gentle friend with whom I bonded over the years. Besides sharing moments of ordinary life, we also took trips together to give inclusion and accessibility trainings. Francis was meek, quick to offer a word of comfort and to joke around with others. He also celebrated well. First of all, he celebrated himself. He said that he liked himself and that he was born with a disability, which he saw as something good. He was an artist and a rocker, proud to be part of a band. Francis also celebrated others. He spoke with love and admiration about his family members. He would let people he hadn't seen for some time know how he wanted to hang out with them. He also used social media regularly to affirm his favorite rock singers and to post good morning messages for his online contacts to read at the start of their day.

Francis's death arrived unexpectedly. One evening he was watching a favorite television show with his housemates before going to bed and the next morning he did not wake up for breakfast. Upon receiving the news of his passing that morning, I went to the house and was there when his body was taken away. In a matter of minutes, his bed was empty and Francis was gone. The room still contained his possessions—his comic books, his posters, his pictures, his clothes, and everything else he left behind—but he no longer was there to enjoy them.

On the day of his passing the atmosphere around the house was surreal; people were in disbelief. His room became a place of prayer, with pictures and objects from his life on his bed to remember him and lit candles around it. His family members, housemates and friends that came to give their condolences could go to his room, write or draw him messages on small cards that they could leave on his bed, and pray as they felt inclined. In the evening, we gathered for a memorial prayer service in the living room, followed a few days later by a church funeral.

Both the prayer service for Francis and his funeral were times of mourning. People were sad, trying to process the loss or at least accept such a sad occurrence. After the initial shock, although we felt sorrow at his death, we also began to celebrate Francis. During a prayer service we shared memories about him, affirmed him by mentioning traits we liked about his personality that were still with us, and we sang a song of blessing for him. At the funeral service, his community of friends was invited to process into the church carrying an object that reminded them of Francis, leaving it at the foot of the altar. Although we mourned and were confused by his abrupt death, we did not stop celebrating him. To this day, his memory and his spirit are still present in community, as well as our affirmation of it.

By drawing out what is good and admirable in the other, we affirm that the light is brighter than the forces of isolation, marginalization, hate, and death. As we build community with others, celebrating and forgiving them, we appreciate and rejoice in their uniqueness, trusting in their gift for the world and letting them know that we believe in them.

Epilogue

When I first encountered Nick, I noticed right away how demonstrative his smile appeared when he was joyful but also his frown when he was upset. A young adult with autism, he could not verbalize his feelings and thoughts, and had uncommon ways of relating to surroundings, but his facial expressions and posture showed great interest in the world around him and sincere engagement with the people in his life.

One afternoon, Nick came to meet me in the community home living room, took my hand and pointed to the floor above. Although I did not know what that meant, I trusted him. I let myself be led as he accompanied me upstairs to the second floor to get a cartoon book, *The Flintstones*, so that I could read it to him. As I began reading the book out loud, he listened attentively and each time I finished a page he would turn to the next. Afterwards, he invited me to watch together his favorite show on the living room's television set—*The Flintstones*, of course. After watching the cartoon for a bit, I picked a theology book from a nearby shelf and started browsing through it. Nick put his hand on it, closed it, looked at me and pointed at the show, which wasn't over quite yet. I was about to get caught up in fancy theological discourses and complex philosophical wording, but Nick called me back to the "Yabba dabba doo!" catchphrase, reminding me of the "little way" of trust. He asked that I be present to him, which made sense to me, as that was precious for him—and for me. Watching an animated sitcom alongside him was enough. Could I trust that?

I often hear of people working on themselves, trying to effect big change in their lives and seeking to "make it"—with themselves, in relationship with others, and in other aspects of their lives. Believing in ourselves and the other, however, may very much be a "little way," as we trust our preciousness and belovedness, letting that free us as individuals and as a people.

Appendix: Questions for Reflection

Below are questions for your reflection, should you wish to use them, divided by chapters. Grounded in the themes of the book, they invite you to engage in self-awareness and I hope will help you in your trust journey. These questions may be used individually or in a group, for personal and/or group reflection.

Believing in Yourself

Who Are We?

1) Ask yourself "Who am I?" What images and/or words come to your mind? Is there one you find to be deeper than the others?

2) What masks do you tend to wear? In what circumstances and why? How can you let go of the masks?

3) In which space, activity or relationship do you sense your authentic self easily coming alive? How does this happen?

Being Ourselves

1) Just being, take one minute to be present where you are. What do you see? What do you hear? If thoughts come to mind, let them pass like a ship at sea.

2) What role does leisure have in your life and what value do you give to it?

3) A fruitful life is life-giving. In what ways have those around you, in the past or present, received life from you?

Loving Ourselves

1) How have you experienced love in your life? Are there any particular images, stories and memories that rise up within you?

2) On the path of love, you might live both easy and difficult moments. What helps you believe in love through ups and downs?

3) How do you like to be loved? Are there practical ways in which you can love yourself in a similar way?

Claiming a Deeper Love

1) What gives you solace?

2) What activities, rituals or practices help you enter peaceful spaces within yourself, beyond or beneath the many voices of the mind?

3) How would claiming your deepest identity as "the beloved" change how you approach yourself and others (if at all)?

Reconciling with Our History

1) What role does your past have in how you perceive a present situation?

2) Drawing from your life experience and wisdom, what would you tell your younger self should s/he ask you for advice during a challenging time?

3) What parts of your history do you need to reconcile with? What supports do you need to do so?

Embracing Our Abilities and Inabilities

1) What are some of your gifts? If you are not able to name them, what are qualities or traits of yours that others have affirmed and appreciated?

2) What are things you can't do or have a hard time doing?

3) Recall one or more practical examples of your abilities and inabilities. In regard to your inabilities, who can help you when you cannot do something? At the same time, when others cannot do something, how can your gifts come to their aid?

Accepting Our Bodies

1) Reflect on a small decision you need to take. Notice how you engage in the decision-making process. Is it mostly "head work," or is it also grounded in your physical sensations?

2) How has your day been thus far? What felt sensations, rather than just ideas, appear as you seek to answer this question?

3) In what concrete ways do you take care and/or can take care of your being?

Following Our Inner Voice

1) Bring to mind a specific decision in which you had a clear sense that the decision came from your conscience. Where did that sense come from?

2) Why might you think it is important to inform your conscience so as to help you decide well?

3) When you make major decisions, what discernment process do you tend to follow? Has that brought good fruit?

Believing in the Other

Encountering the Other

1) Who do you miss when they are gone?

2) How do you move from simply meeting to encountering others?

3) Who are some of the important people in your relational history? Why are they important?

Being with the Other

1) What contexts and spaces help you be present to others?

2) How do you know if your relationships with others are fruitful (life-giving)?

3) What place does silence have in your being present to others?

Meeting the Other at the Margins

1) What part of yourself do you marginalize? Do you do it consciously or unconsciously?

2) What barriers have you built around yourself that you'd like to move past?

3) Who is at the margins of your family, your neighborhood, and your society? How can you foster unity?

Celebrating the Other

1) In observing the world around you, when have you ever experienced a sense of wonder and appreciation?

2) What place does affirmation have in your communication with others?

3) What are the ways, both small and big, through which you can meaningfully celebrate the people you know?

Endnotes

1 Henri J.M. Nouwen, *With Open Hands* (New York: Ballantine Books, 1972), xi.

2 Raffaele Morelli, *L'Unica Cosa Che Conta* (The Only Thing That Matters) (Milan: Mondadori, 2010), 81.

3 Ken Sedlak, *Why God Loves Us...No Matter What* (Liguori: Liguori Publications, 2007), 13.

4 Ralph Waldo Emerson and Henry David Thoreau, *Nature Walking* (Boston: Beacon Press), 85.

5 Cecile Andrews, *Slow is Beautiful: New Visions of Community, Leisure and Joie de Vivre* (Gabriola Island: New Society Publishers, 2006), 145.

6 Josef Pieper, *Leisure, the Basis of Culture* (South Bend: St. Augustine's Press, 1998), 32.

7 Ibid.

8 Lennard J. Davis, "Constructing Normalcy: The Bell Curve, the Novel, and the Invention of the Disabled Body in the Nineteenth Century, " *The Disability Studies Reader*, 2nd ed., ed. Lennard J. Davis (New York: Routledge, 2006), 6.

9 Carl G. Jung, *Modern Man in Search of a Soul* (New York: Houghton Mifflin Harcourt Publishing Company, 1993), 235.

10 Daniel J. O'Hanlon, S.J., "Integration of Christian Practices: A Western Christian Looks East," *Studies in the Spirituality of Jesuits* XVI, no. 16 (1984): 10.

11 Quoted in Anselm Grün, *Il Piccolo Libro della Vita Buona* (The Little Book of the Good Life), trans. Anna Bologna (Brescia: Editrice Queriniana, 2008), 163.

12 St. John of the Cross, *John of the Cross: Selected Writings*, ed. Kieran Kavanaugh, O.C.D. (Mahwah: Paulist Press, 1987), 89.

13 Henri J.M. Nouwen, *The Inner voice of Love: A Journey Through Anguish to Freedom* (New York: Image Books, 1999), 29.

14 Henri J.M. Nouwen, *Life of the Beloved: Spiritual Living in a Secular World* (New York: The Crossroad Publishing Company, 2002), 30.

15 Fiona Myers, Alastair Ager, Patricia Kerr, and Susan Myles, "Outside Looking In? Studies of the Community Integration of People with Learning Disabilities," *Disability & Society* 13, no. 3 (1998): 393.

16 Henri J.M. Nouwen, *Bread for the Journey: A Daybook of Wisdom and Faith* (New York: HarperCollins, 2006), 86.

17 David Richo, *Daring to Trust: Opening Ourselves to Real Love and Intimacy* (Boston: Shambhala Publications, 2010), 158.

18 Nikos Kazantzakis, *Report to Greco*, trans. Peter A. Bien (New York: Simon & Schuster. 1965), 43.

19 Anselm Grün and David Steindl-Rast. *Faith beyond Belief: Spirituality for Our Times* (Collegeville: Liturgical Press, 2016), 145.

20 Pope Francis. *The Joy of the Gospel: Evangelii Gaudium (*United States Conference of Catholic Bishops, 2013), p. 51.

21 Ibid., 140.

22 Dietrich Von Hildrebrand, *The Heart: An Analysis of Human and Divine Affectivity* (South Bend: St. Augustine's Press, 2012), 42-43.

23 Marcel Proust, *In Search of Lost Time. Volume I, Swann's Way, Vol.* I, trans. Charles K.S. Moncrieff and Terence Kilmartin (New York: Modern Library, 2004), 60-63.

24 Ibid., 64.

25 Nancy L. Eiesland, *The Disabled God: Toward a Liberatory Theology of Disability* (Nashville: Abingdon Press, 1994), 100.

26 Germain Grisez, *Christian Moral Principles* (Quincy: Franciscan Press, 1983), 78.

27 Antonio Corduba, *De Conscientia,* Bk. III, qu. IV, quoted in Henry Newman, *A Letter Addressed to the Duke of Norfolk on Occasion of Mr Gladstone's Recent Expostulation* (London: Pickering, 1875), 66.

28 Sedlak, 9.

29 Augustine of Hippo, "Homily 7 on the First Epistle of John," *From Nicene and Post-Nicene Fathers, First Series, Vol.* 7, ed. Philip Schaff (Buffalo: Christian Literature Publishing Co.), 504.

30 Dennis Linn, Sheila Fabricant Linn, and Matthew Linn, *Healing the Future: Personal Recovery From Societal Wounding* (Mahwah: Paulist Press, 2012), 141.

31 John R. Sachs, *The Christian Vision of Humanity: Basic Christian Anthropology* (Collegeville: Liturgical Press, 1991), 107.

32 Buber, M. (1970). I and thou (1st ed.). New York, NY: Touchstone.

33 Erik Trinkaus and Pat Shipman, *The Neandertals: Changing the Image of Mankind* (New York: Knopf, 1992), 340-341.

34 Xavier LePichon, "Ecce Homo: Accogliere la Sofferenza È il Segno della Nostra Umanità" (Behold Humanity: To Welcome the Suffering Is the Sign of Our Humanity), *Magis. Quaderno di Spiritualità*, no. 1 (2009): 7.

35 Blaise Pascal, *Pensées*, trans. John Warrington (London: Dent and Sons, 1973), 70.

36 David G. R. Keller, *Oasis of Wisdom: The World of the Desert Fathers and Mothers* (Collegeville: Liturgical Press, 2005), 143.

37 Henri J. M. Nouwen, *Out of Solitude: Three Meditations on the Christian Life* (Notre Dame: Ave Maria Press, 2004), 38.

38 Italo Calvino, *Invisible Cities*, trans.William Weaver (Orlando: Harcourt, Inc., 1974), 87.

39 Hafiz, *The Gift: Poems by Hafiz, the Great Sufi Master* (New York: Penguin, 1999), 39.

40 Teresa, of Avila, *Interior Castle*, trans. Edgar A. Peers (Radford: Wilder Publications, 2008), 24.

41 Anselm Gruen, *Heaven Begins Within You* (New York: The Crossroad Publishing Company, 1999), 25.

42 Robert E. Sinkewicz, *Evagrius of Pontus: The Greek Ascetic Corpus* (Oxford: Oxford University Press, 2003), 230.

43 William G. Justice and Warren Lambert, "A Comparative Study of the Language People Use to Describe the Personalities of God and Their Earthly Parents," *The Journal of Pastoral Care* 40, no. 2 (June 1986): 170.

44 See Dennis Linn, Sheila Fabricant Linn, and Matthew Linn, *Healing Spiritual Abuse and Religious Addiction* (Mahwah: Paulist Press, 1994).

45 Dennis Linn, Sheila Fabricant Linn, and Matthew Linn, *Good Goats: Healing Our Image of God* (Mahwah: Paulist Press, 1994), 50.

46 Simone de Beauvoir, *The Second Sex*, trans. Constance Borde and Sheila Malovany-Chevallier (New York: Vintage Books, 2011), 763.

47 Thomas Merton, *Conjectures of a Guilty Bystander* (New York: Image Books, 2009), 153-155.

New City Press

New City Press is one of more than 20 publishing houses sponsored by the Focolare, a movement founded by Chiara Lubich to help bring about the realization of Jesus' prayer: "That all may be one" (John 17:21). In view of that goal, New City Press publishes books and resources that enrich the lives of people and help all to strive toward the unity of the entire human family. We are a member of the Association of Catholic Publishers.

www.newcitypress.com
202 Comforter Blvd.
Hyde Park, New York

Periodicals
Living City Magazine
www.livingcitymagazine.com

Scan to join our mailing list
for discounts and promotions
or go to www.newcitypress.com
and click on "join our email list."

www.ingramcontent.com/pod-product-compliance
Lightning Source LLC
Chambersburg PA
CBHW060054100426
42742CB00014B/2824

* 9 7 8 1 5 6 5 4 8 3 4 8 4 *